Contents

658.3 TMO
.40Z INT

658.45. QMI
45 GOW

331.34 YOU

~~331 34 12 ASM~~

~~303 78 655 ERA~~

ills

hrs

at it is embedded, relating directly to a
; transferable to the workplace; learner-
s built in; students are encouraged
.

o teams can be time-consuming if they miss
a fundamental element within Business
e for some); some expressed a wish for more
fficult for some to manage. (n.b. the portfolio
s in 2000 / 2001).

vere:

eful

Youth in Transit

A profile of 16-25 year olds

LESLIE J. FRANCIS
London Central YMCA

Gower

Published by
Gower Publishing Company Limited,
Gower House, Croft Road, Aldershot, Hampshire GU11 3HR, England.

British Library Cataloguing in Publication Data

Francis, Leslie J.
   Youth in transit.
   1. Youth -- England -- London -- Attitudes
   I. Title
   303.3'8 (expanded)   HQ799.G7

   ISBN 0-566-00530-1 /

YOUTH IN TRANSIT

t.

Foreword

Co-operation between London Central YMCA and the Leverhulme Trust Fund created a unique opportunity for a social psychologist to devote three years to the fascinating study of young people aged between 16 and 25 years at the city centre. It was my privilege to take advantage of this opportunity. During those three years I was able to assemble an extraordinarily rich data base. Youth in Transit is the attempt to make available to a wider audience some of my findings.

London Central YMCA was responsible not only for initiating this project, but also for drawing together a body of wise and helpful academics from a variety of disciplines to act as a research advisory group under the chairmanship of Professor David Miller (Middlesex Hospital Medical School). Serving on this group were Professor Garth Plowman (London School of Economics), Dr. Richard Farmer (Westminster Medical School), Alan Beattie (University of London, Institute of Education), John Burrows (University of London, Extra-Mural Department), John Sutcliffe (University of Cambridge, Department of Education), together with three members of staff from London Central YMCA, Leslie Adams, Colin Mawby and Geoffrey Palmer. I owe a deep debt of gratitude to all of them for giving so generously of their time and advice.

My thanks are also due to the staff of London Central YMCA for their assistance throughout the project and for making my period with them so enjoyable and worthwhile, to the many men and women who have co-operated in the research by completing my questionnaire, to John Irwin of the Gower Publishing Company for his help in designing this book, to Carole Boorman for so patiently and competently typing the final manuscript, and to Keith Clark for assistance with proofreading.

Great Wratting Rectory   Leslie Francis

December 1981

1 Introduction

Youth in Transit is the account of a research project initiated by London
Central YMCA and sponsored by the Leverhulme Trust Fund during the
late 1970's and early 1980's into the attitudes, values and needs of young
people between sixteen and twenty-five years of age at the centre of
London. The project is an essay in pure social research in the sense that
it sets out to provide a detailed, objective and unbiased account of the
young people encountered through the sampling procedure. At the same
time, the project is an essay in applied social research in the sense that
it is providing information of direct relevance to those working with that
age group through the provision of accommodation, education, recreation,
counselling or leisure facilities.

BACKGROUND

The research project's life began in the minds of the staff and management
of London Central YMCA. It is necessary, therefore, to give some brief
background to this development. London Central YMCA traces its own
origin back to 1844 when George Williams founded a society for 'improving
the spiritual conditions of young men engaged in the drapery and allied
trades'[1]. London Central YMCA first opened buildings on its present
central London site on the corner between Great Russell Street and
Tottenham Court Road in 1912. During the late 1960's and early 1970's
the association began to re-think and to re-design its central London
operation. This involved the demolition of its early twentieth century
building and the development of totally new plant. At the same time the
association decided that it was necessary to take a fresh look at the
people with whom it was making contact in the inner city, giving special
attention to the careful researching of the attitudes, values and needs of
its target population, young people between the ages of sixteen and
twenty-five years. The object in doing this was not only to increase the
effectiveness of its own operation, but also to stimulate academic debate
regarding the contribution of such research to work among young people in
general.

London Central YMCA's new premises, George Williams House, were
opened in stages during 1976 and 1977. As well as providing hotel and
hostel accommodation for over eleven hundred people, the London Central
YMCA Centymca Club operates leisure and recreational facilities for
more than seven thousand members. The club facilities include on site
an art room, audio studio, billiards room, chapel, chess room, dance studio,
lounges, coffee bars, meeting rooms, photographic studio and dark room,
practice halls, reading room, a language school, sauna, solarium, sports

hall with climbing wall, squash courts, swimming pool and weight training room. Off site, in South London, the club also has a good sports ground offering facilities for soccer, cricket and tennis. The full-time professional staff employed by the club, together with a number of skilled volunteer leaders, offer a wide range of recreational, cultural, creative and educational programmes.

It is important to recognise from the outset that the membership of London Central YMCA is open to women and not just to men, to people of all ages over the age of sixteen and not just to the young, to people of all religious faiths or none and not just to Christians. Within a very short space of time after opening London Central YMCA had built up its membership quota of seven thousand and ever since there has been a lengthy waiting list. It is this total membership which has provided the sampling frame for the present research study.

The collection of the data on which this report is based began in January 1979 when the new premises of London Central YMCA were already entering their third year of life. By this stage the life of the club had settled down. The research facilities provided by the club provided an ideal social laboratory from which to develop a widely based study. As the subsequent analysis will adequately demonstrate, the membership includes a very wide range of men and women of all ages from a variety of racial, creedal, educational and social backgrounds. It is for this reason that the results of the project will prove to be of broad interest and of considerable value beyond London Central and the YMCA movement itself to the wider field of those concerned with the service of youth.

The present book is a complete and self contained account of the central thrust of the research project. It does not, however, exhaust the potential of the data base. This is the case for two reasons. First, the analysis is restricted to the young people in the sample aged between sixteen and twenty-five years, although this age group in fact represents well under half the respondents. Analysis is concentrated on this age group because of the importance of these years in the development of the individual and the relevance of the analysis for youth work in general. Work is already in progress to produce the companion study on the next age group, the period of young adulthood between the ages of twenty-six and thirty-nine years. Second, the kind of analysis presented is of a simple and straightforward nature. The aim has been to afford the non-technical reader direct access to what young people are themselves saying, and to do so with the minimum of interpretation and evaluative overlay. The quality of the data bank also permits the use of more sophisticated statistical techniques and the accompanying theoretical interpretations, but it is not the aim of this book to engage in this kind of discussion. In effect, what I am doing is to present the reader with much of the raw material as a basis both for their own reflection and from which they will be in a strong position to test my further analysis and future speculation.

DESIGN

When I was appointed to translate London Central YMCA's abstract research concept into a concrete research protocol I was given a broad brief. The brief was to chart the attitudes, values and needs of the young people aged between sixteen and twenty-five years who come into contact with the association, and to do so in such a way that the results of the project would both promote at the highest possible level the academic discussion of the needs of young people during that critical period of development while in transit from being children at school to becoming established in adult society, and also be directly of help in the structuring and formulation of its policies. In order to sharpen the focus of the project I decided to occupy the first year accomplishing three preliminary but essential tasks.

First, I made a thorough search of the literature to survey what had already been achieved by way of research in the area of the study of young people between the ages of sixteen and twenty-five years. The information service at the National Youth Bureau in Leicester, friends at the University of London Institute of Education and the members of the London Central YMCA research advisory group were all very helpful. I do not propose to take space here to provide a thorough review of the literature. My general conclusion was that work in this area had not been particularly plentiful, apart from research in specific areas like the effect of college environments [2] or the transition from school to work or unemployment [3]. I failed to find an existing framework of research which was broadly enough based and onto which I could constructively build. I decided, therefore, that it was necessary to make an original start.

Second, I talked with a wide variety of people who were concerned with working among young people in the sixteen to twenty-five year age group. I began with the staff of London Central YMCA and the National Council of YMCA's. Then I began to make contact with other people within the wider context of the voluntary and statutory youth services. What, I continually asked, would these people wish to learn from a new research initiative in this area? What did the professionals want to know about the attitudes, values and needs of young people between the ages of sixteen and twenty-five years? These conversations helped to define the precise areas within which the research could be most useful to the practical field of youth work.

Third, I settled down alongside young people, both within the London Central YMCA and elsewhere. I listened to the issues that they were discussing and the matters that were important to them. In this way I became much more aware of the areas which the project would need to research if it was to provide an accurate and thorough description of what the young people wanted to say themselves about their attitudes, values and needs. At the same time, I became aware of the language through which I would be able to explore these matters clearly and unambiguously.

This initial process of exploration also served to make me more aware of the kind of research report for which there was a real need in the area of work among young people between the ages of sixteen and twenty-five years. It seemed to me that at the present stage in the development of youth work among this age group, the primary and urgent need was for a study which would describe and define the attitudes and values generally held by young people. Moreover, such a study needed to be presented by the social psychologist in a non-technical manner and with a directness which would enable the youth worker to recognise that the study was speaking about the young people with whom he or she was actively involved. This book is to be seen, therefore, as providing the definitions and descriptions of the attitudes and values of young people which can become the foundations on which subsequent studies and the more sophisticated analysis of the present data can build. I came to realise that without these foundations of description and definition, the study of this age group at the present time would remain unrelated to the practical functions it was seeking to serve.

FOCUS

As a result of the literature review and the discussions both with those engaged in youth work and with young people themselves, the decision was taken to focus the research project on twelve key psychological areas. Focus on these twelve areas would both allow the young people to speak clearly for themselves regarding the issues on which they wish to make themselves heard and also provide those working among young people with key information about their attitudes, values and needs. I propose to provide a brief introduction to these twelve areas in the order in which they are subsequently reviewed throughout the rest of the book. The labels employed to describe the content of these areas are well-being, worry, values, self image, beliefs, morals, law, politics, society, work, leisure and counselling.

Well-being   The concept of well-being is employed to sum up the individual's overall attitude to life as a kind of global index of life satisfaction [4]. The kind of questions I decided to ask under this heading were general questions concerned with the young person's overall response to life, and especially with their overall response to life at the city centre. More specific questions concerned with the satisfaction they receive from individual aspects of their lives, like their work, relationships and leisure, I decided to deal with separately. This decision is not based on a theoretical or empirical argument about the way in which the concept well-being should be employed in social psychology, but on the practical basis of attempting to convey a clear and disciplined map of the way in which young people experience and talk about their lives. Young people who believe themselves to be experiencing a high level of general well-being in the sense in which I am employing the construct, tend to say things like 'I find life really worth living' or 'I feel my life has a sense of purpose'. Young people who believe themselves to be experiencing a low level of general well-being tend to say things like 'I am worried that I cannot cope', 'I often feel depressed' or 'I have sometimes considered taking my own life'. In this sense the negative aspect of the concept of well-being alerts us to the incidence of suicidal thoughts among young people and the possible risks of attempted suicide [5].

Worry   Related to the concept of well-being, but kept distinct for the purposes of analysis is the notion of worry. Listening to their conversations, key areas of worry for the young people which emerged from time to time are the personal ones concerned with their work, or lack of it, their debts, their relationships with other people, their sex lives and their health. I decided also to explore the level of anxiety among young people about such issues as mental breakdown, cancer and growing old. I also wanted to know what proportion of young people would claim to be worried in a general sense about 'the world situation'.

Values   The concept of values is being employed to look at the areas and
issues to which the young person ascribes worth or importance. Three
main value areas are selected for attention. These are economic values,
including such notions as work, home ownership, making, spending and
saving money; personal values, including such factors as family, friends,
home and self; and social values, including religion, morality and politics.

Self image   The term self image is used to assess the kind of image of
themselves which the young people are concerned to project to the
researcher. A major problem in such areas as attitude research concerns
the way in which both questionnaire respondents and interviewees may
tend to project an untruthful but socially desirable image of themselves [6].
A range of standard questions has been developed in the research
literature to assess the extent to which such tendencies are operative in
a given population. The kind of areas often explored in this context are
those identifying characteristics which are usually deemed socially
unacceptable but which at the same time few people can truthfully deny[7].
The precise issues I decided to include were telling lies, breaking promises,
stealing, feelings of jealousy and resentment, admitting to mistakes and
taking advantage of others.

Beliefs   Beliefs, like values are important factors underlying the young
person's response to life. In particular the churches have become much
more conscious during the past few years of the importance of listening
to what young people themselves are saying about their own religious
beliefs [8]. In this section, therefore, I decided to examine what the
young people believed about God, Jesus Christ, life after death, reincarnation, the church, the Bible and religious education in schools. At the
same time I wanted to examine what they believed about such things as
their horoscope and the part played by luck in their lives, as well as their
response to such issues as the existence of intelligent life on other planets.

Morals   During the 1960's a revolution took place in the young person's
moral attitude and values [9]. The area of morals remains one of central
importance both to young people themselves and to those working with
them. Under this heading three main areas of morality were selected for
attention. These are sexual ethics, including the young person's attitude
towards contraception, extra-marital sexual intercourse and homosexuality;
the sanctity of life, including issues like abortion, euthanasia and war; and
attitude towards alcohol and drugs like marijuana and heroin.

Law   The next section moves on from an examination of the young
person's attitude towards morality to look at their attitude towards the
law. The purpose of this section is to identify the extent to which young
people today regard themselves as essentially law abiding and the extent to
which they are willing to hold aspects of the law in contempt. The kind of
issues I decided to review in this area included the young person's attitude
towards the evasion of custom duties, the dishonest completion of tax
returns, travelling without a ticket on public transport, the disobeying of
speed limits and parking restrictions and the issue of drinking and driving.

Politics   Politics is a vast area. Under this heading the research project
limited itself to three primary issues. First, I wanted to examine the
young person's involvement in politics and their confidence in the

policies of the major political parties. Second, I wanted to gauge their
attitude on key political issues like nationalisation, education, the health
service, trade unions, immigration, the Common Market and international
trade. Third, I wanted to assess their perceptions of different sectors of
society by examing their attitude towards the pay claims of groups like
nurses, doctors, policemen, carworkers and miners.

Society   Under the concept of society, I proposed to examine the young
person's attitude towards specific features of life in today's society. I
wanted to assess their perceptions of current trends in such areas as the
crime rate, the educational standard of schools, the efficiency of the
health service, the divorce rate, the availability of abortion, violence on
television, pornography and credit card facilities. At the same time, I
was interested in ascertaining the extent to which they registered concern
about such issues as pollution, nuclear war, the third world, inflation,
unemployment and homelessness.

Work   The attitude of young people towards their work is a matter of
central importance both to themselves and to their employers. In this
area I decided to look at the satisfaction which young people derived
from their work, their reason for working and their ambition to do well
at work.

Leisure   The young person's attitude towards leisure is becoming a matter
of increasing importance given the sharp increase in youth unemployment[10].
In this area I wanted both to assess the attitude held by young people to
their leisure in general and to provide a detailed picture of their
preferences for different leisure time activities. In particular, I wanted to
listen carefully to what they were saying about their level of interest in
the fifty or so specific leisure time activities or facilities provided within
London Central YMCA itself, since their reactions to these facilities and
activities would be of direct relevance both to the YMCA and to other
recreation and leisure centres in planning and developing the use of their
resources in terms of plant, equipment and personnel.

Counselling   The final area to be embraced is that of counselling.
There is a growing awareness of the need for counselling facilities for
young people, especially in the inner city [11]. London Central YMCA,
among other agencies, is responding to this need not only by providing
counselling facilities within the association for residents and members, but
also by opening on its premises an 'off the street' counselling service for
young people in general. There are two kinds of information I wanted to
collect in this area. First, I was interested in the young people's
perceptions regarding their own counselling needs and the counselling
needs of their contemporaries. Second, I was interested in ascertaining
the kind of people whom the young people would consider approaching
for counselling purposes.

METHOD

Having determined the focus of the project, in terms of specifying the
specific areas of attitudes, values and needs to be researched, the next
important decision concerned the selection of the appropriate research
method. There is a very clear relationship between the selection of a
research method and the kind of information which can be collected [12].

The three basic methods available to me were the observation, interview and questionnaire techniques. Both the interview and the questionnaire techniques permit a further choice to be made between open-ended and closed questions. After much discussion, the self-completion questionnaire method was selected making use primarily of closed questions. This technique seemed to have six important advantages. It is possible to collect data from a much larger sample of respondents. It is possible to ask a number of questions over a wide range of topics, defining each question in a precise way. It is possible to build into the questionnaire objective methods of testing for response bias, carelessness and deliberate falsification. The self-completion questionnaire enables the respondents to give time to the project when they are away from the London Central YMCA building. This is important because some of the members soon find that the time which they are able to spend in the building itself quickly becomes committed to various aspects of the programme. Once a questionnaire has been carefully constructed, it becomes possible to replicate the study easily. This could be of importance in two ways. It would be possible now to repeat the study in London Central YMCA in a specific number of years time and to begin to chart the way in which the attitudes and values of young people in central London are changing over time. Similarly, it would be possible to repeat the study at any time in other cities in England or elsewhere in order to build up an exact picture of the differences and similarities between the London situation and the situation elsewhere. Finally, if questionnaires are carefully designed with the possibilities of certain scaling properties in mind, once a large data base has been assembled, it is possible to re-analyse the data file from a number of different perspectives in order to explore the full possibilities of precise measurement and the careful construction of prediction models.

The questionnaire itself evolved, as questionnaires do, slowly and through a whole series of discussions and pilot testings. Draft forms of the questionnaire were discussed with people concerned with the voluntary and statutory youth services and with academics concerned with survey work and educational research. Pilot applications of the questionnaire were tried first in schools and among college classes so as to avoid contaminating unnecessarily the population from whom the final sample would be drawn. Finally, the questionnaire was tested among members of the London Central YMCA itself.

The final version of the questionnaire was designed to collect information about the twelve key aspects of the young person's psychological development already outlined above. Each of these twelve areas was studied by means of a battery of precise questions. In the questionnaire these questions were randomised so that the items relating to the distinct areas did not cluster together. After the questionnaire had been designed and carefully tested, the research programme itself was ready to start. The strategy was to give the questionnaire to everyone who joined London Central YMCA or renewed their membership, whatever their age. The questionnaire was given personally to the members who came to the club reception desk to pay their fee, and sent by post to the few who paid postally. Each questionnaire was numbered, and a record card was kept of the name and address of the person to whom each questionnaire was given or sent.

The numbering system was designed simply to enable us to know who had not returned the questionnaire so that reminder letters could be mailed to them. The respondents were assured that once their questionnaire had been returned, the number would be detached from it so that it would not be possible to associate individual questionnaires with the names of the individuals who had completed them. Completion of the questionnaire was in no way compulsory. In fact the questionnaire was not given out with the membership application forms but at the time when the person had already been accepted into membership, paid a membership fee and received a temporary membership certificate. Members were invited to co-operate in the project and to bring their questionnaires back to the club reception desk when they came in person to receive their membership card. 40.4% of those to whom questionnaires had been given returned completed questionnaires in this way without any further request being made for them to do so.

A month or so after the questionnaire had been given out and after the membership card had been collected a reminder letter was sent to those members who had not returned their questionnaire. This reminder letter resulted in a further 7.9% returning their questionnaire. Finally, six weeks or so after the first reminder letter had been sent, a second copy of the questionnaire was posted to those who had still not replied together with a stamped addressed reply envelope. This second reminder letter drew completed questionnaires from a further 9.0% of the members. Thus, all told there was a response rate of 57.3%. This percentage refers to the questionnaires which were totally completed and useful in the analysis. The return of partly completed questionnaires was regarded as synonymous with a refusal to co-operate in the project and therefore those who submitted partly completed questionnaires were counted among the non-respondents. In terms of the average response rate to questionnaires completed in the respondents' own time and regarding which there is no compulsion to reply, this represents an exceptionally good return, particularly in view of the length of the questionnaire, the sensitivity of some of the items and the fact that the sample included a considerable number of people for whom English was a second language.

RESPONDENTS

Over the period of time that was available for data collection, the response rate of 57.3% resulted in there being available for analysis 1,085 completed questionnaires from the young people aged between sixteen and twenty-five years. I propose now to describe this sample of 1,085 cases carefully in terms of the information available from their completed questionnaires.

Recently, London Central YMCA organised a small street survey in various parts of London [13]. About four hundred passers-by were stopped and asked a few questions about the YMCA. The overall impression which came across was that most people think of the YMCA as existing for the young rather than the old, for men rather than for women, and only for those who can subscribe to the Christian faith. For example, less than one-third of those questioned thought that the YMCA was open to women as well as to men, and another third was unsure whether non-Christians could use the YMCA or not. A close look at the age, sex and religious affiliation of the respondents makes quite a contrast with this popular image.

<u>Age</u> The sixteen to twenty-five year olds make up just under forty per cent of the total membership, and the rest of the members are older. In an age which makes so much of the generation gap and the need to provide specialist and separate facilities for the young, it is very significant that in London Central YMCA so many people in their late teens and early twenties want to be associated with a club where more than sixty per cent of the members are over twenty-five, and more than forty per cent are in fact over thirty.

A closer look at the sixteen to twenty-five age group reveals that only a small proportion are under the age of eighteen. There is a fairly even distribution between the ages of eighteen and twenty-five, with the twenty to twenty-one year olds being slightly less well represented than the eighteen to nineteen year olds and the twenty-two to twenty-three and twenty-four to twenty-five year olds. In fact only 8.5% of the 1,085 sixteen to twenty-five year olds are aged between sixteen and seventeen, while 23.5% are eighteen or nineteen, 18.4% are twenty or twenty-one, 24.9% are twenty-two or twenty-three and 24.7% are twenty-four or twenty-five years of age.

<u>Sex</u> From being an all male organisation, the YMCA is growing steadily into an association which caters equally for men and women. The achievement of a balance between the sexes is being realised most satisfactorily among the association's target population of the sixteen to twenty-five year olds. Now 43.2% of this age group are women.

<u>Religion</u> Replies to the questionnaire not only confirmed that the membership of the YMCA was neither predominantly young nor predominantly male, they also clearly indicated that only about one third of the members claimed allegiance to any religious faith. In response to the question 'Are you a practising member of a religious group (in London or elsewhere)?', 64.8% firmly answered that they were not.

27.1% of the respondents claimed allegiance to the Christian faith, and a further 8.1% claimed allegiance to one of the other world religions. The two largest non-Christian groups were Muslim with 3.4% of the respondents and Jewish with 2.8% of the respondents. There were also seven Buddhist, five Hindu and five Sikh members. Of the 27.1% of the respondents who claimed to be practising Christians, the largest group (12.4%) said that they were members of the Church of England and the next largest group (11.1%) were members of the Roman Catholic Church. The other Christian denominations were represented by only a few members each. There were seven Methodists, five Baptists, four Quakers, four Pentecostalists, three members of the United Reformed Church, eight Greek Orthodox and one Russian Orthodox member. Four claimed to be Christians without belonging to any denomination. There was also one Mormon, one Jehovah Witness, one Spiritualist and one member of a meditation group.

<u>Nationality</u> London Central YMCA has a truly international membership. 35.8% of the members were born outside England, Scotland, Wales or Northern Ireland. Only twenty-five members refused to divulge the country of their birth. The 380 foreign born members describe themselves as coming from 63 countries. Table 1.1 sets out the country of birth and the numbers of members mentioning each country. The three places most strongly represented are Malaysia, Iran and Hong Kong. These figures are consistent with the fact that in 1980 Malaysians were the largest

national group of overseas students in the United Kingdom.

Table 1.1 Country of Birth

Country	N	Country	N
Algeria	1	Malaysia	33
Argentina	4	Malta	2
Australia	8	Mauritius	1
Bahrain	2	Mozambique	1
Belgium	2	Netherlands	2
Brazil	1	New Zealand	3
Brunei	1	Nigeria	17
Canada	5	Pakistan	7
China	4	Peru	3
Cyprus	15	Portugal	4
Denmark	2	Rhodesia-Zimbabwe	3
Egypt	3	Singapore	4
Eire	11	South Africa	7
France	10	Spain	1
Germany	16	Sri Lanka	4
Ghana	5	Sudan	3
Gibraltar	2	Sweden	1
Greece	10	Switzerland	5
Guyana	2	Syria	1
Hong Kong	22	Taiwan	1
India	15	Tanzania	2
Indonesia	14	Thailand	2
Iran	26	Trinidad and Tobago	1
Iraq	6	Turkey	4
Israel	2	Uganda	3
Italy	14	USA	20
Jamaica	8	Uruguay	1
Jordan	3	Venezuela	5
Kenya	8	Vietnam	1
Kuwait	1	West Indies	8
Lebanon	2	Zambia	3
Malawi	2		

37.1% of the foreign members had been living in Great Britain for more than five years. Nearly two-thirds, therefore, were relative newcomers to the country. 15.6% had been here less than a year, and a further 23.3% had been here between one and three years. London Central YMCA thus seems to be providing a base for foreigners who have newly arrived in London to work or to study. At the same time with such a truly international membership London Central YMCA has a unique opportunity to further international understanding.

Looking beyond the young people themselves to the country of their parents' birth, we find that 87 countries are represented. A number of the young people had themselves grown up in England as first generation citizens. In particular, within this category there are small groups with Polish, Jamaican, Indian or Southern Irish backgrounds.

London   The majority of the young members of London Central YMCA are relatively new to London life. Less than one-third had lived in London all their lives. 57.1% had lived in London for less than five years, while 15.8% of them had lived in London for less than one year. The YMCA appears to be an important centre through which new relationships can be made by those young people who are new to the city.

The respondents who had not lived in London all their lives had moved there from a number of different backgrounds. 20.7% had come from another major city centre or major city suburb, and another 14.8% had come from a large town of more than 50,000 inhabitants. On the other hand, a third of the members had come to London from much smaller communities. 6.3% had come from small villages of less than 500 inhabitants; 10.2% had come from large villages, and the remaining 16.7% had come from small towns of less than 50,000 inhabitants. These different groups are likely to have quite different expectations and perceptions of living in central London.

The 420 respondents who had moved to London from another part of England had in fact come from all over the country. Only one county of England was not represented among the membership, namely Shropshire. As might have been expected, the counties most represented were those in the South East, Essex, Kent, Surrey and Sussex. There seems to be a movement from these counties to the city centre itself. Next came Hampshire with 28 members, Yorkshire with 26 and Lancashire with 22.

Accommodation   More than three quarters of the respondents live within a ten mile radius of the centre of London. 15.3% live within a mile of London Central YMCA itself, and a further 37.4% live between one and four miles away. For these young people, the whole range of city centre facilities are on their doorstep. Although a number of young people must commute into London to work or to study, only 10.7% of the membership live more than fourteen miles away. London Central YMCA's main work is among the young people resident in central London rather than among the commuters.

Over three-quarters of the young respondents are living in houses or flats with other people. 11.0% report that they are living with their own family, while 30.1% are living with their parents and a further 33.2% are living in accommodation shared with others who are not members of their own family. For the young people sharing accommodation with their parents or with others it is often important to have somewhere else to go in order to relax with friends. On the other hand, 13.6% live alone or in bedsits and for these London Central YMCA may provide an alternative to isolation. A further 12.1% live in hostels.

Marital Status   As is likely to be inferred from the previous section on accommodation, the majority of the sixteen to twenty-five year old members of London Central YMCA are in fact single. Only 6.9% are or have been married, while a further 10% are living together. Moreover, 8.1% of the married members are now separated or divorced. The young men and women most attracted to the facilities of London Central YMCA are primarily those who do not have established homes and families of their own.

Employment   At the time of completing the questionnaire, the ratio

11

between the members who were employed and those who were students was about two to one. 69.3% were in employment, while 30.7% were students. Often it is the case that students and workers do not come together for their leisure time activities. What London Central YMCA appears to be in a position to achieve is a very desirable mix between these two different groups of young people.

Of those in employment, 83.2% were in full time employment, 5.1% in part time employment and 11.7% were self-employed. The respondents include a most remarkable range of people working in different jobs. In the building industry, for example, there were three plumbers, three carpenters, three electricians, a mason, a builder's labourer, five civil engineers, eight surveyors and some architects. There were eighteen hairdressers, seventeen shop assistants, two bakers, four printers, thirteen waitresses and five barmen. There was a taxi driver, a train guard and a railway signalman. There were nine telephonists and eighty-two secretaries. There were five policemen, one commercial traveller, nine school teachers, two university teachers and fifteen solicitors. In the medical field there were two doctors, thirteen nurses, one pharmacist, one optician, three chiropodists and one physiotherapist.

Unemployment   The problem of unemployment among young people is an issue of growing concern. London Central YMCA has among its members a considerable number of young people who have had experience of unemployment. 31.5% of the respondents had in fact experienced periods of unemployment during the past two years. For the majority of them, this experience of unemployment had been between one and six months in duration. However, 4.8% of the respondents had been unemployed for the whole of the previous two years, and another 5.4% had been unemployed for up to twelve months of that period.

Social Class   On the basis of information about the respondents' work it is possible to assign them to socio-economic groups in accordance with the five social gradings proposed by the Office of Population, Censuses and Surveys in 1970 [14]. According to this classification, professionals like doctors, accountants, solicitors and clergymen, are assigned to social grade one. Semi-professionals, like teachers, social workers, journalists and entertainers are assigned to social grade two. Social grade three includes bus drivers, clerks, secretaries and electricians. Social grade four includes postmen, machine operators, bricklayers and bus conductors. Finally, social grade five includes the unskilled manual labourers, porters, and messengers. In looking at the questionnaire responses in relationship to this categorisation it was, of course, necessary to omit students and the unemployed for whom there was no basis on which to assign a socio-economic grade.

Analysis of the social grading of occupation indicates that the membership of London Central YMCA seems weighted towards social grades one and two with just over 50% of the respondents coming into this category. This is likely to be in part the result of the fact that the range of employment available in central London, including the universities, hospitals and technical institutions, attracts skilled and professional people. The membership of London Central YMCA naturally reflects the environment in which it is placed.

Qualifications   A number of the young people who come to central London do so to further their education, either as full time students or as part time students in association with earning their living. The academic standard of the membership of London Central YMCA is, therefore, quite high. 2.3% of the respondents already hold a higher degree, and an additional 15.8% hold a first degree. Some of these are now studying for their second degree. All except for 14.5% of the respondents have at least some O levels, and nearly half (46.7%) have attained some A levels. All except 18.4% of the respondents have received some full time education after the minimum school leaving age of sixteen. 29.8% left full time education when they were seventeen or eighteen, and a further 9.7% left at the ages of nineteen or twenty.

As far as non-academic qualifications are concerned, 9.9% of the membership have a secretarial qualification, 5.8% have a business or commercial qualification and 14.0% have a professional qualification.

Income   Income was assessed in response to the question 'What is your average take home pay?' in terms of pounds sterling per week. Take home pay was interpreted to include student grants. The replies show that the respondents' affluence in terms of their weekly income varies greatly. While one group of 11.6% of the members received more than £80 per week, another 11.6% received less than £30 per week. Between these two extremes, 13.1% received between £30 and £40, 22.5% received between £40 and £50, 20.6% received between £50 and £60, 13.6% received between £60 and £70 and 7.1% received between £70 and £80. These income figures need to be assessed in light of the fact that central London tends to be an expensive place to live in terms of accommodation, food and travel.

The Questionnaire   The very last question in the questionnaire was designed to discover how the respondents felt about filling in the questionnaire itself. They were asked to rate their level of agreement with the simple statement 'I have enjoyed filling in this questionnaire' on the five point scale of agree strongly, agree, not certain, disagree, disagree strongly. Only 17% of the total sample said that they had not enjoyed completing the questionnaire. There was no difference in the response to this question between men and women or between British and foreign members. There was, however, a significant difference in response according both to age and to social class. The younger members enjoyed completing the questionnaire more than the older members. 72.8% of the sixteen and seventeen year olds enjoyed the exercise compared with 57.7% of the twenty-four and twenty-five year olds. The graph depicting the change between these two ages almost assumes the shape of a straight line. 67.9% of those in social class four enjoyed completing the questionnaire, compared with 57.5% in social class one, 59.7% in social class two and 63.7% in social class three.

ANALYSIS

The main substance of this book, chapters two through eleven, is concerned with the analysis of the replies to the questionnaire of the 1,085 young respondents. Chapter two begins the analysis by reviewing the overall responses of the whole group of young people. In this chapter, their responses are reviewed to the items which constitute each of the twelve areas embraced by the survey, namely, well-being, worry, values, self image, beliefs, morals, law, politics, society, work, leisure and counselling. The items organised to define these twelve areas are printed in full in this chapter in order to establish firmly the empirical meaning given to each key concept. The following nine chapters review these twelve key areas of the young person's development in relationship to nine factors which seem to have an important relationship with them. These subsequent chapters can be read in any order, depending upon the reader's main interest and concerns. However, chapter two really needs to be read first because it sets out to clarify the rationale according to which the attitudes discussed in the subsequent chapters are organised.

Chapter three reviews the differences in the responses of men and women. In so doing this analysis contributes to our understanding of the psychology of gender differentiation [15]. It is of importance for those operating leisure, recreational and educational facilities for young people of both sexes to appreciate the way in which their values, attitudes, interests and needs differ. It is particularly important for an association which started life in the mid-nineteenth century as an all male institution and continued as such for one hundred years, to understand how in the last part of the twentieth century it can serve with equal effectiveness the needs of men and women.

Chapter four reviews the differences in the responses of those in their late teens and those in their early twenties. It is important for those working with young people during the period of rapid development and change between the school leaving age and their growth into adult society to know how the twenty-five year olds respond differently from the eighteen year olds, and how both of these age groups can work within the same association with each other, as well as with older people. In particular, although London Central YMCA is an association which has a special concern for young people, it needs to be remembered that it has no age limit on its membership and that in fact over half its members are aged over twenty-five.

Chapter five reviews the differences in the responses of students and young workers. Often it is the case that leisure, recreational and educational facilities, either intentionally or unintentionally, cater for young people either who are in employment or who are students. Much of the previous study of the development of values and attitudes in the immediate post-school period has been concerned with the student population. This YMCA study provides a unique opportunity to compare students' and workers' values in the same inner city environment in the English context [16].

Chapter six examines the responses of the young people who have experienced periods of unemployment and compares them with those who have not experienced unemployment. Unemployment among young people has become a matter of urgent concern, while as yet too little is known about the effect of unemployment on young people [17]. Those working with young people in contexts like London Central YMCA need to become increasingly aware of the social and psychological implications of the experience of unemployment, and to explore ways of helping the young people in this situation [18].

Chapter seven compares the responses of the young people born in Britain with those born overseas. The young people in London belong not so much to England as to a cosmopolitan city. It is increasingly important to understand how the most fundamental values and outlooks differ between people brought up in different cultures. Only in this way is it possible for an international youth agency like the YMCA to foster international understanding [19]. It cannot be assumed that it is sufficient simply to bring together young people of different cultural backgrounds without offering them some ways of exploring and learning to understand each other's cultural differences. This chapter also draws attention to the particular needs of those who have newly arrived in England. It is, for example, important to recognise the distinctive needs of the young people who have newly arrived from overseas as students in London University or the surrounding colleges.

Chapter eight reviews the relationship between attitudes and social class. It is important for the management and professionals who operate leisure, educational and recreational facilities for young people to understand the way in which social class may function as a significant determinant of attitudes, values and the way in which people wish to spend their leisure time and to assure that leisure facilities are provided with the implications of this factor clearly in mind.

Chapter nine reviews the differences in the responses of those who live in different forms of accommodation. The young people who come into contact with London Central YMCA adopt a number of different patterns of accommodation; some live at home with their parents, others in bedsits, halls of residence, hostels, shared houses or communes. Little is known regarding the extent to which styles of accommodation are related to attitudes and values, and the different kinds of problems and stresses associated with each. Information of this nature should help the YMCA in assessing its role in providing hostel accommodation in the city centre[20]. It should also be of particular interest to the colleges and employers who bring young people to London and need to consider the problems of helping them to find appropriate places to live.

Chapter ten reviews the relationship between educational qualifications and attitudes. Educational qualifications are increasingly important in the labour market, but little is known about the fundamental relationship between educational levels and attitudes and values. By bringing together young people of widely different educational backgrounds, from those who have no qualifications to those who have already completed higher degrees, London Central YMCA is in a unique position to study the barriers that may exist between people of different educational levels.

Chapter eleven examines the responses of those who are practising members of certain Christian denominations and compares them with those who are not. A cosmopolitan city attracts young people of all religious faiths and none. It is important to understand the influence both of faith and of lack of faith on attitudes and values. It is of special importance for an organisation like the YMCA which has an explicitly Christian foundation to appreciate the differences in values and attitudes of those who adhere to the Christian faith and those who do not. This analysis also provides the churches with an opportunity to assess their influence on the attitudes and values of their young adherents [21].

Thus, chapters three through eleven are concerned with assessing whether the responses of recognisable groups, like men and women or students and workers, are in fact significantly different in the statistical sense.

Statistical tests of significance have been calculated in relationship to the responses of all the groups between which comparisons are made. Analysis of variance, t-tests and chi square significance tests have been applied as appropriate within different situations [22]. In order to simplify the presentation of material the results of these significance tests are not quoted in the text. The convention adopted is to report differences only if the five per cent probability level has been reached. In cases where this level has not been reached, it is reported that the groups do not significantly differ. Throughout these nine chapters the percentage responses of the different groups are reported either in the text or through the tables. I have tried to report all the significant percentages, but not to present the same statistics more than once in both text and tables. The reason for this has been to achieve a brief, economical and yet thorough coverage of a large quantity of detailed information, while at the same time highlighting the more interesting statistics through the visual presentation of the tables. It is, therefore, necessary to read the text and the tables in close association with each other.

Each of the chapters three through eleven follows the same pattern of reviewing in turn the differences between the groups under discussion in respect of the twelve areas of well-being, worry, values, self image, beliefs, morals, law, politics, society, work, leisure and counselling. The reader who wishes to trace any one of these twelve areas through the nine chapters is enabled to do so through the cross referencing provided by the index. For example, the index makes it easy to follow the way in which well-being is related to sex differences, age differences, social class differences, levels of education, religious affiliation, and so on.

After the previous chapters have reviewed the different characteristics of the groups outlined above and accomplished the proper task of statistical generalisations, chapter twelve turns attention to just seven of the individual members, and presents in some detail their unique personal profiles. The questionnaire used to collect data in this study enables us to categorise respondents and to make generalisations about specific groups. At the same time it preserves the uniqueness of each individual and enables us to return to the data file in order to pick out the way in which each individual differs from the groups to which he or she most closely belongs. Space would never permit a thousand detailed studies: but a few case studies can serve to illustrate the richness of the data and remind us that, beneath the useful generalisations, we are the whole time dealing with uniqueness and individuality. In the last analysis, one of the greatest benefits of sociological generalisations about young people is the way in which these generalisations help us to gain insight into the individuals whom we know and among whom we work. These personal profiles demonstrate the richness of the information collected by the project. They are presented last because they will make most sense after the reader has become familiar with the rationale according to which the whole sample has been studied.

NOTES

[1] For fuller information on the life of George Williams and the YMCA see J.E. Hodder Williams, The Life of George Williams, Hodder and Stoughton, London 1906; Clyde Binfield, George Williams and the YMCA, Heineman, London 1973; C.P. Shedd, History of the World Alliance of YMCA, SPCK, London 1955.

[2]   J. McLeish, Student's attitudes and College Environments, Institute of
        Education, Cambridge 1970; A.W. Astin, Four Critical Years, Jossey-
        Bass Publishers, San Francisco 1977.
[3]   G. Holland, Young People and Work, Manpower Services Commission,
        London 1977; C. Murray, Youth Unemployment: a social-psychological
        study of disadvantaged 16 - 19 year olds, NFER, Slough 1978.
[4]   P. Warr, 'A study of psychological well-being', British Journal of
        Psychology, 69, 111 - 121, 1978.
[5]   Elizabeth R. McAnarney, 'Adolescent and young adult suicide in
        the United States', Adolescence, 14, 765 - 774, 1979.
[6]   A.L. Edwards, The social desirability variable in personality
        assessment and research, Dryden Press, New York 1957.
[7]   D. O'Donovan, 'An historical review of the lie scale - with particular
        reference to the Maudsley Personality Inventory,' Papers in Psychology,
        3, 13 - 19, 1969.
[8]   Bernice Martin and R. Pluck, Young People's Beliefs, General Synod
        Board of Education, London 1977; British Council of Churches Youth
        Unit, Young People and the Church, British Council of Churches,
        London 1981.
[9]   D. Yankelovich, The New Morality, McGraw-Hill, New York 1974.
[10]   M.A. Smith and A.F. Simpkins, Unemployment and Leisure: A review
        and some proposals for research, Centre for Leisure Studies, Salford
        1980.
[11]   T. Wylie, Counselling Young People, National Youth Bureau,
        Leicester 1980.
[12]   C.A. Moser and G. Kalton, Survey Methods in Social Investigation,
        Heinemann, London 1971; G. Hoinville, R. Jowell et al (eds),
        Survey Research and Practice, Heinemann, London 1978.
[13]   L.J. Francis, 'The YMCA and young people today', YMCA World
        Communique, 2(3), 5 - 6, 1980; 'The YMCA Off the Record',
        Youth in Society, 37, 42, 1979.
[14]   See Office of Population Censuses and Surveys, Classification of
        Occupations, HMSO, London 1970.
[15]   E.E. Maccoby and C.N. Jacklin, The Psychology of Sex Differences,
        Stanford University Press, Stanford, CA 1974; J.E. Parsons (ed),
        The Psychobiology of Sex Differences and Sex Roles, Hemisphere,
        Washington, DC 1980.
[16]   In the American literature a similar comparison is afforded by
        D. Yankelovich, The New Morality: a profile of American Youth in
        the 1970's, McGraw-Hill, New York 1974.
[17]   Marie Jahoda, 'The impact of unemployment in the 1930's and the
        1970's,'Bulletin of the British Psychological Society, 32, 309 - 314,
        1979; G. Shepherd, 'Psychological disorder and unemployment', Bulletin
        of the British Psychological Society, 34, 345 - 348, 1981; J. Hayes
        and P. Nutman, Understanding the Unemployed, Tavistock Publications,
        London 1981.
[18]   The National Council of YMCA's is taking a very positive initiative in
        the field of youth unemployment through its Training for Life scheme;
        see Graham Hobbs, 'Training for Life', Youth in Society, 33, 7 - 9,
        1979.
[19]   L.J. Francis, 'Educating International Understanding', Adult Education,
        53, 99 - 101, 1980.
[20]   Susan Quinn, Home or Away, National Council of YMCA's, London
        1979.

[21]   M.P. Smith and R.M. Lee, <u>Roman Catholic Opinion</u>, University of Surrey, Guildford 1979.

[22]   All statistics were computed by the SPSS package version H release 8; see N.H. Nie, C.H. Hull, J.G. Jenkins, K. Steinbrenner and D.H. Bent, <u>Statistical Package for the Social Sciences</u>, McGraw-Hill, New York 1975.

2 Global view

The purpose of the present chapter is to give an overview of the attitudes and values of the whole group of young people aged between sixteen and twenty-five years who responded to the questionnaire. This discussion is organised into the twelve areas introduced in chapter one, namely well-being, worry, values, self image, beliefs, morals, law, politics, society, work, leisure and counselling. These headings are being employed as a way of organising the information which the questionnaire was designed to collect. There is no suggestion that these areas are homogeneous or independent psychological variables in the sense, for example, of empirically derived factor scales. This chapter will make clear the precise meaning and importance of each of the twelve areas by listing the specific attitude statements which provide their operational definition.

WELL-BEING

The concept of well being is employed to sum up the individual's attitude to life as a kind of index of life satisfaction [1]. It signifies the extent to which the individual feels that life is on his or her side. Twelve questions are asked to gauge different aspects of this notion of well-being, ranging from the positive affirmation that 'I find life really worth living', to the desperation of 'I have sometimes considered taking my own life'. Under the concept of well-being particular attention is given to the extent to which the sixteen to twenty-five year olds feel at home in the inner city, or the extent to which they feel alienated or isolated.

The first impression given by table 2.1 is that the vast majority of the young people enjoy a great deal of personal well-being, at least superficially speaking: 84.2% agree that they find life really worth living. However, when the respondents are invited to probe their feelings a little more deeply and to examine their sense of purpose in life, this feeling of well-being emerges neither as secure nor as widespread as it first appears. Although 84.2% say that they find life really worth living, the proportion of those who feel certain that their lives have a sense of purpose falls to 73.1%. Another indication of the superficiality of this feeling of well-being for some is given by comparing the proportions of those who agree strongly with these two statements. Thus, only 22.6% agree strongly that their lives have a sense of purpose, compared with the 35.7% who agree strongly that life is really worth living. This means that more than a quarter of the young people are not certain of a sense of purpose for their lives at all, or else clearly deny it.

Table 2.1   Well-being

	AS%	A%	NC%	D%	DS%
I find life really worth living	35.7	48.5	12.4	3.0	0.5
I feel my life has a sense of purpose	22.6	50.5	20.6	5.3	0.9
I like to have a lot of people around me	13.7	45.0	20.9	18.5	2.0
I find crowds oppressive	9.1	30.0	22.0	32.6	6.3
I tend to be a lonely person	4.1	18.1	14.4	45.3	18.2
I feel no one knows me	3.2	11.5	12.6	47.1	25.7
I often long for someone to turn to for affection	15.1	34.4	14.4	29.2	6.9
I often long for someone to turn to for advice	5.1	19.9	15.3	40.7	18.9
I often feel depressed	7.2	21.2	15.2	40.8	15.6
I am worried that I cannot cope	2.2	11.0	13.1	47.2	26.4
I feel I am not worth much as a person	1.2	5.7	12.1	38.6	42.5
I have sometimes considered taking my own life	2.6	16.5	7.2	21.1	52.5

KEY AS   agree strongly
     A   agree
     NC   not certain
     D   disagree
     DS   disagree strongly

Turning attention to the negative dimensions of the concept of well-being, the questionnaire explored the feelings of loneliness and desperation experienced by the respondents. Socially, life in the inner city represents a paradox. On the one hand, it is crowded with people. On the other hand, it can really accentuate feelings of loneliness. Only 58.7% of the young people in the inner city claim that they actually like to have a lot of people around them, and of these only a very small proportion (13.7%) agree strongly that this is the case. In fact 39.1% say that they find crowds oppressive and 22.2% of the young people say that they tend to be lonely. For 14.7% this isolation and loneliness is so great that they feel quite certain that no one knows them, while a further 12.6% are not certain whether anyone really knows them or not. Looked at another way, only 63.5% are confident that they are not lonely and 72.8% are confident that there is someone who really knows them. The feeling of isolation is thus quite widespread among this group of sixteen to twenty-five year olds, and there is consequently a longing after others to turn to for affection or advice. Half of the sample claim that they often long for someone to turn to for affection, and a quarter claim that they often long for someone to turn to for advice.

Feelings of depression affect more than a quarter of the sample: 28.4% admit that they often feel depressed, while only 56.4% seem sure that they do not often feel depressed. At the same time, 13.2% are worried that they cannot cope, and 6.9% consider that they are not worth much as a person.

The proportion of this age group who have felt so depressed at one time or another that they have considered taking their own lives is very high. Suicidal thoughts are openly admitted by 19.1% of the sample, and firmly denied by only 73.7%. In other words at least one fifth of the sample has found life so intolerable at some point that they have thought of ending it all.

WORRY

The review of well-being has suggested that one person in every four often experiences periods of depression, anxiety or worry. What, then, are the main sources of worry and anxiety for these young people? Listening to their conversations, the key areas seem to be personal ones concerned with work, money, relationships and health, but also there is the more pervading anxiety about the world in which they are living. The questionnaire replies enable us to quantify the importance of these respective areas.

Table 2.2   Worry

	AS%	A%	NC%	D%	DS%
I am worried about the world situation	12.6	52.1	23.8	9.9	1.6
I often worry about my work	11.8	33.8	13.8	33.1	7.5
I am worried about my debts	4.3	17.9	11.6	43.8	22.4
I am worried about my relationships with other people	6.1	16.3	13.8	44.8	19.0
I am worried about my sex life	3.9	11.8	12.7	44.8	26.8
I am worried about my health	5.4	19.5	10.2	44.2	20.6
I am worried about growing old	8.0	18.6	19.8	32.9	14.5
I am worried that I might have a breakdown	1.7	8.3	12.3	40.0	37.8
I am worried that I might get cancer	4.3	28.8	21.9	34.5	10.6

The first observation to emerge from table 2.2 is that more of the sixteen to twenty-five year olds consider that they are worried in a general sense about the world situation than are worried about specific personal issues. Two-thirds of them (64.7%) are ill at ease about the world in which they live. They feel that they are living in a problematic world and that there is little they can do to change the situation.

Turning attention to the more specific and personal areas of worry, work emerges as the greatest concern for this age group, and money takes second place. Thus, nearly half (45.6%) worry about their work, and nearly a quarter (22.2%) are worried about their debts. Life in the inner city is both competitive and expensive. Work is a real sense of anxiety and so is money. One in four of the young respondents has already found that it is all too easy to live beyond his or her income and is now discovering the anxiety that comes from being in debt.

After work and money, the other two main centres of worry for the young people are concerned with relationships and health. Again, about one in four of the young respondents (22.4%) claims to be worried about his or her relationships with other people, and 15.7% are worried about their sex life. Relationships remain an important area of concern for the sixteen to twenty-five year olds.

Amid the physical and mental strains of life in the inner city, 24.9% of the young people report that they worry about some aspect of their health. Moreover, one in ten is worried that the pressures of life might lead to a breakdown. Looking at their health in a broader perspective, one in four (26.6%) is worried about growing old, and one in three (33.1%) is worried that he or she might get cancer.

VALUES

The concept of values is being employed to look at the areas and issues to which the young person ascribes worth or importance. The questionnaire responses enable us to compare the proportion of young people who ascribe worth to different key aspects of life. The three areas embraced are economic values, including money and work, personal values, including self, family and friends, and social values, including religion, morality and politics.

Table 2.3   Values

	AS%	A%	NC%	D%	DS%
Saving money is important to me	20.1	51.2	13.0	14.3	1.6
Making money is important to me	16.7	49.6	16.0	15.2	2.5
Spending money is important to me	12.5	42.4	19.2	23.1	2.8
It is important for me to own my own house	30.6	43.3	13.4	11.7	1.0
My appearance is important to me	32.8	56.2	7.1	3.4	0.5
What people think of me is important to me	21.5	49.7	12.4	12.3	4.1
Friends are important to me	68.2	27.2	2.9	1.2	0.6
My home and family are important to me	50.6	40.2	4.7	3.6	0.9
My work is important to me	35.7	53.2	6.8	3.9	0.5
Religion is important to me	11.7	20.0	29.7	27.6	11.6
Moral values are important to me	28.9	51.6	13.8	4.4	1.3
Having a good time is more important than anything else	11.0	21.5	21.5	39.6	6.3
Politics is important to me	11.9	35.0	24.3	20.5	8.2

The overall impression gained from table 2.3 is of hardworking and serious-minded young people earnestly trying to build a future for themselves. An important insight into the economic values of the young people comes from the comparison of their responses to the three questions about money, namely concerning making money, spending money and saving money. While 66.3% consider that making money is important to them, a slightly higher percentage (71.3%) consider that saving money is important. By way of comparison, only 54.9% consider that spending money is an important part of their lives. The first priority of the young people is saving money for the future. The second priority is making money, and only then comes spending money as third in priority. Another index of their investment in the future is the fact that three out of four of the young people consider that it is important for them some day to own their own house.

Nine out of ten of the young respondents place a high value on their work. It is interesting to note that considerably more of them consider that their work is important than consider that making money is important, that is 88.9% compared with 66.3%. The young people obviously do not work simply for the money. There is much more for them in their work than merely the financial reward.

Exploring the dimension of personal values, the vast majority of the sixteen to twenty-five year olds attach considerable importance to their family and friends. In fact, 95.4% say that friends are important to them, while 68.2% feel strongly that this is the case. At the same time, 90.8% say that their home and family are important to them, while 50.6% feel strongly that this is the case. Looked at another way, only 1.8% disagree that friends matter to them, and only 4.5% disagree that their homes and families are important.

The majority of sixteen to twenty-five year olds also attach considerable importance to their appearance and to their reputation. Thus, 89.0% consider that their appearance is important to them, and 71.2% are concerned about what other people think of them. Only 3.9% deny the importance of their appearance and only 16.4% deny the importance of their reputation.

What kind of social values do these young people espouse? Basically, the sixteen to twenty-five year age group is a generation which has little time for religion, but it is not one without a strong sense of the importance of moral values. Less than one-third of the respondents consider that religion is important to them, while well over another third are convinced that religion has no importance to them. The remaining third have not made up their minds. On the other hand, 80.5% consider that moral values are important to them, and only 5.7% clearly dismiss moral values as unimportant. The majority of the young people say that they take seriously the question of moral values, and that they value highly their own code of right and wrong. Nearly one half disagree with the hedonistic principle that having a good time is more important than anything else, although one in every three accepts this as a general principle on which to order his or her life.

As far as politics is concerned, almost half of the young people (46.9%) agree that politics is important to them compared with 28.7% who consider it unimportant. Meanwhile, the remaining 24.3% have not made up their minds whether politics is important to them or not. This indicates that one in four of the young people is not yet committed to any valuation of the importance within his or her life of the social values of religion and politics. They are neither committed to these values, nor prejudiced against them.

SELF IMAGE

The section on values suggests that the majority of sixteen to twenty-five year olds take themselves seriously and are concerned about what other people think of them. This section on self image looks at the young person's response to seven items which often figure in lie scales or indices of social desirability [2]. A close analysis of the responses to the items presented in table 2.4 helps us to gauge the extent to which the young people are concerned to project a good image of themselves, as well as giving an indication of the way in which they really see themselves. Responses to these items also provide a test against which we can judge the veracity of the answers to the rest of the questionnaire.

Table 2.4   Self Image

	AS%	A%	NC%	D%	DS%
I have never told a lie	1.2	3.1	7.6	50.4	37.7
Sometimes I have been jealous of others	12.7	64.2	9.7	10.4	3.0
Sometimes I feel resentful when I do not get my own way	5.7	57.9	14.2	20.7	1.5
I have never broken my promise	4.6	17.5	22.9	47.7	7.2
Sometimes I have taken advantage of other people	8.4	51.2	18.8	17.9	3.7
I have never stolen anything in my life	13.1	17.6	11.8	46.9	10.5
I am always willing to admit when I make a mistake	14.6	54.1	16.0	13.9	1.4

The overall impression is that the young people possess a fair degree of insight, and that they have been willing to present an accurate image of themselves through the questionnaire. The vast majority are not afraid or ashamed to admit to themselves or to others that they may have some socially undesirable characteristics. This indicates that, in spite of the tensions and strains under which they may be living, they basically retain a great deal of confidence in themselves as people. They do not need to exaggerate their good qualities in order to win the approval of others [3].

Thus, only 4.3% claim that they have never told a lie, and only 13.4% deny that they have sometimes been jealous of others. The majority admit to being resentful when they do not get their own way and to breaking promises. The majority know that they have taken advantage of people, and they openly admit to having stolen something in the course of their lives.

Interestingly, 68.7% consider that they are always willing to admit when they make a mistake. The replies to the other questions suggest that this answer is not an exaggeration made just to impress. The majority of the young people seem to set out to deal truthfully, even when the truth can set them in a bad light.

BELIEFS

What kind of beliefs do the sixteen to twenty-five year olds hold about the world in which they live? Is it a world created and directed by some supernatural being or not? Are these young people on their own in the world or are their lives guided by some greater force? Already we have seen that 64.8% claim to belong to no religious group and only 31.7% agree that religion is important to them. This section looks more closely at the respondents' belief system.

Although only 35.2% of the sample claim to be practising members of a religious group, 57.6% of the sample would describe themselves as theists who claim that they believe in God. A further 28.4% are agnostics who are not certain whether they believe in God or not, while only 14.0% are atheists who claim not to believe in God. Interestingly, a slightly higher proportion of the theists are strongly committed to their belief position than the percentage of the atheists who are strongly committed to their position. 37.0% of the atheists hold their atheistic position strongly compared with 43.0% of the theists who hold their belief in God strongly.

Table 2.5   Beliefs

	AS%	A%	NC%	D%	DS%
I believe in God	25.0	32.6	28.4	8.8	5.2
I believe that Jesus Christ is the Son of God	21.1	23.6	36.2	8.5	10.6
I believe in life after death	17.1	25.9	39.1	11.3	6.7
I believe in reincarnation	8.6	15.0	41.1	16.9	18.4
The Bible seems irrelevant for life today	6.9	17.2	35.6	30.3	10.0
The church seems irrelevant for life today	5.4	18.3	37.3	31.4	7.5
I take an active part in church	1.8	4.2	10.0	48.8	35.2
I think religious education should be taught in schools	9.0	48.9	27.1	10.9	4.1
I believe there is intelligent life on other planets	20.3	32.3	37.4	6.1	3.9
I believe in my horoscope	3.6	14.7	33.0	27.4	21.2
I believe that luck plays an important part in my life	9.3	40.2	24.3	21.7	4.5

Although 13.0% less of the sample believe in the divinity of Jesus Christ as compared with those who believe in the existence of God, this still produces a comparatively high proportion (44.7%) who are willing to ascribe to the traditional test of Christian orthodoxy by assenting to the claim 'I believe that Jesus Christ is the Son of God'. Thus in terms of what they believe, 44.7% of the young people can be termed Christian, as compared with the 27.1% who claim to belong to a Christian denomination. Considerably more uncertainty is associated with the issue of belief in the divinity of Jesus Christ than with the existence of God. Whereas one in

four of the sample is agnostic about belief in God, one in three is agnostic about the divinity of Jesus Christ.

Religious belief sets human life against the perspective of the eternal. In order to assess the young person's awareness of this perspective, two questions were asked, one from a traditional Christian standpoint and another from a non-Christian standpoint. The responses clearly show that the young people have not made up their minds on this religious perspective. More than one in three remain uncertain about both the Christian and the non-Christian interpretations: 39.1% do not know whether they believe in life after death or not, and 41.1% do not know whether they believe in reincarnation or not. Where there is a significant difference is in the proportion who believe in these two different religious positions. 43.0% believe in life after death, compared with 23.6% who believe in reincarnation.

The next two questions provide an opportunity to test the attitude of young people towards Christianity as represented through the church and the Bible. About one in four are flatly dismissive of both the church and the Bible, with 23.7% saying that the church seems irrelevant for life today and 24.1% saying that the Bible seems irrelevant for life today. A considerably higher proportion, about 40.0% in each case, disagree with these statements. Although 38.9% clearly think that the church has some relevance for life today, only 6.0% claim to take an active part in the church. Again, a very significant feature of the data is that one young person in three has not made up his or her mind whether the church and Bible are relevant for today or not. The door is far from closed against traditional Christian belief and practice.

Another section of the questionnaire complements the present information about the respondents' religious beliefs and attitudes by asking questions about their religious practices. The three religious practices reviewed were Bible reading, attending a place of worship and praying. The precise questions were 'When did you last read the Bible by yourself?', 'When did you last attend church, synagogue, mosque or other place of worship – apart from occasions like weddings or funerals?' and 'When did you last pray by yourself?' In fact, 6.9% had never been to a place of worship, 14.2% had never prayed and 22.0% had never read the Bible. Looked at another way, however, quite a high proportion of the young people claimed some recent contact with religion. Within the last week 4.7% had read the Bible, 9.5% had attended a place of worship and 30.9% had prayed. Within the last twelve months, 30.4% had on some occasion read the Bible, 53.8% had attended a place of worship and 61.9% had prayed. Thus although two thirds of the sample would claim quite clearly not to belong to a religious group and only one quarter would claim to be Christians, over half have had some contact with a place of worship during the past year and nearly two thirds have prayed. There seems to be a much greater openness among young people to the religious dimension than is displayed through their adherence to a religious group.

Similarly, a basic interest in religious matters is indicated by the response to the question 'I think religious education should be taught in schools'. Only 15.0% firmly think that religious education should not be taught. A further 27.1% are not certain whether it should be taught or not, but the majority (57.9%) assert that it should be taught.

Turning attention away from traditional religious beliefs and practices, the questionnaire included three questions on the wider area of belief in the supernatural and supraterrestrial. To begin with, the world of science fiction has established a popular mythology regarding the existence of intelligent life on other planets. Whether or not such intelligent life in fact exists is a matter of belief rather than established fact. It is interesting to note that more than half of the young people (52.6%) place their belief in the existence of intelligent life on other planets, only 5% less than the proportion who believe in God. Moreover, 20% hold to this belief strongly. The question of whether or not there is intelligent life on other planets is not one which is likely to have much bearing on the young person's day to day life. There can be little urgency for them to think through this issue and formulate a view on it, so it is particularly significant that only 9.0% more are agnostic about life on other planets than are agnostic about belief in God. Finally, just 4.0% less reject the possibility of life on other planets than reject belief in God.

The question of horoscopes is an interesting one, since most newspapers and magazines carry a horoscope and many people read them. Nearly half of the young people reject belief in their horoscope, more than three times the number who reject belief in God. One in three are uncertain whether to believe in their horoscope or not, while only 18.3% in fact believe in their horoscopes. While only a small proportion of these young people accept belief in their horoscope, a much larger number are content to talk in terms of their lives being guided by chance. One in every two of the sample claims that luck plays an important part in his or her life, while only one in four confidently rules out this possibility.

MORALS

Under the concept of morals the survey included questions about three primary issues, namely sexual ethics, the sanctity of life and attitudes to drugs and alcohol. The earlier section on values shows that 80.5% of the young people regard moral values to be important to them. This does not mean that young people are holding in high regard the traditional moral norms of society. It means that their own moral code is one which they take seriously.

The liberalisation of heterosexual ethics among young people is now well established. The period of indecision is over. As compared with the religious issues reviewed in the previous section, very few young people have not made up their minds where they stand on heterosexual issues. Less than 10.0% check the uncertain category on questions concerning contraception and extramarital intercourse. Only 3.0% believe that contraception is wrong; 5.9% believe that it is wrong for an unmarried couple to live together, and 10.1% believe that it is wrong to have sexual intercourse outside marriage. The vast majority accept these practices as morally right. Moreover, about two thirds of those who accept these practices as morally right feel strongly about their acceptance of them.

By way of comparison, the young people are not adopting such an unequivocably liberal view towards homosexual ethics. Whereas 79.9% of the young people are convinced that it is not wrong to have sexual intercourse outside marriage, only 57.5% are convinced that the practice of homosexuality is not wrong. There is also greater indecision among the young people on the homosexual question than on the heterosexual questions. 17.8% of the members are not certain where they stand on homosexuality as compared with 9.9% who are uncertain about extramarital intercourse. This reflects a wider social ambivalence towards homosexual practice. Society has yet to give a decided answer to this whole question. Finally, one in four of the members considers the practice of homosexuality to be wrong, compared with the one in ten who considers sexual intercourse outside marriage to be wrong.

Table 2.6   Morals

	AS%	A%	NC%	D%	DS%
I think contraception is wrong	1.1	1.9	8.9	24.7	63.4
I think it is wrong for an unmarried couple to live together	2.1	3.8	5.8	34.0	54.3
I think it is wrong to have sexual intercourse outside marriage	4.4	5.7	9.9	29.9	50.0
I think the practice of homosexuality is wrong	13.4	11.3	17.8	33.9	23.6
I think all war is wrong	37.2	24.2	17.1	16.0	5.6
I think abortion is wrong	5.8	8.6	16.6	34.0	35.1
I think euthanasia (mercy killing) is wrong	9.7	14.0	29.8	32.4	14.0
I think it is wrong to use heroin	48.6	30.3	11.3	6.4	3.3
I think it is wrong to use marijuana (hash or pot)	19.8	18.3	18.8	26.0	17.0
I think it is wrong to become drunk	10.9	20.9	17.1	39.7	11.5

Regarding the sanctity of life, a very high proportion of the young people (61.4%) consider that all war is wrong. Moreover, nearly two thirds of those who think that all war is wrong feel strongly about the matter. This strong feeling may reflect the growing strength of such movements as the CND and the popular appeal of pacifism to today's young people.

Some interesting differences exist between the young person's response to the ideas of abortion and euthanasia. Abortion is much more clearly acceptable to the young than euthansia. The young people find it less objectionable to contemplate the termination of a life which has not yet become self-supporting than the termination of a mature life, apparently even if that life is threatened by infirmity and suffering. Whereas 69.1% accept abortion as morally acceptable, only 46.4% accept euthanasia as morally acceptable. There is also considerably more uncertainty about the issue of euthanasia: 29.8% have not yet made up their minds about euthanasia as compared with 16.6% who have not yet made up their minds about abortion. On balance, 14.4% think abortion is definitely wrong and 23.7% think euthanasia is definitely wrong. Whereas the majority of those who think all war is wrong feel strongly about the issue, the majority of those who think abortion or euthanasia is wrong do not feel strongly about it.

It is interesting to explore young people's attitudes to the use of drugs, since this reflects their attitude to the law as well as their moral code. Although the possession of both marijuana and heroin is illegal, the young people make a clear distinction between the morality of the use of hard and soft drugs. The vast majority of them consider the use of a drug like heroin to be morally wrong, while many more of them find the use of a drug like marijuana to be morally acceptable. Thus, only 9.7% consider that it is not wrong to use heroin, compared with 43.0% who believe that it is not wrong to use marijuana. Similarly, fewer have not made up their minds about heroin as compared with marijuana. Four out of every five of the young people consider that it is wrong to use heroin: two out of every five consider it is wrong to use marijuana.

Alcohol remains socially much more acceptable than drugs. Just over half of the young members (51.2%) consider that it is not wrong to become drunk. However, it still remains the case that one out of every three members considers drunkenness to be morally wrong.

LAW

Some young people see the law as a fundamental and necessary aspect of the ordering of society, while others see the law as a sign of a hostile and dominating authority. Are the majority of young people rebelling against the law, or are they willing to co-operate with the law by adopting law abiding attitudes? The aim of this section is to test this question in relationship to three specific aspects of the law regarding which young people frequently have to make their own practical decisions. The three areas are travelling on public transport without a ticket, the paying of taxes and custom duties, and the obeying of motoring laws.

Table 2.7   Law

	AS%	A%	NC%	D%	DS%
It is not wrong to travel without a ticket if you are not caught	4.4	16.6	14.6	47.0	17.4
There is nothing wrong in bringing an extra bottle of spirits through the customs if you are not caught	8.7	34.8	18.0	30.6	7.9
I think tax returns should be filled in with complete honesty	9.5	43.3	24.2	18.5	4.5
There is nothing wrong with drinking and driving if you can get away with it	1.0	4.2	5.5	29.5	59.8
I think speed limits should be strictly obeyed	16.7	44.8	17.3	18.0	3.2
I think parking restrictions should be strictly obeyed	9.0	37.3	27.1	22.2	4.4
There is nothing wrong in selling cigarettes to children under the legal age	2.1	6.6	7.4	31.8	52.0

The first question reviews the young person's attitude towards travelling on public transport without a ticket. The majority of young people are law abiding and honest in their attitudes in this area. Two out of every three argue that it is wrong to travel without a ticket, even if they are not caught. In fact only 21.0% would consider fare dodging to be permissible.

The next two questions review the young person's attitude towards paying taxes and customs duties. The first point to emerge is that the young people seem less scrupulous about evading custom duties than they are about evading public transport fares. Whereas only 21.0% would consider travelling without a ticket to be permissible, more than twice that number (43.5%) consider it permissible to bring an extra bottle of spirits through the customs. The second point to emerge is that just over half the young people (52.8%) consider that tax returns should be filled in with complete honesty, while only 23.0% openly deny this.

The next three questions look at different aspects of the young person's attitude towards motoring laws. They compare the young person's attitude towards parking restrictions, speed limits, and drinking and driving. The young person's responses towards these three questions clearly reflect the different degrees of seriousness they attribute to each. To begin with, 89.3% consider that drinking and driving is wrong, and the majority of them hold to this view strongly. 61.5% think that speed limits should be strictly obeyed, but the majority of them do not hold to this view strongly. By way of comparison, only 46.3% consider that parking restrictions should be strictly obeyed, while only 1.0% of them hold strongly to this view.

Another illuminating way of comparing responses to these three motoring issues is to examine the proportion of the young people who opt for the uncertain response in each case. Only 5.5% have not made up their minds on the drinking and driving issue, while 17.3% have not made up their minds on the speed restriction issue, and 27.1% have not made up their minds on the parking question. The young people seem to have made up their minds on the issues that seem to be matters of more urgent concern, but on the less urgent issues they remain more open minded and probably allow the context to be determinative in any given situation.

This section contains one further question designed to gauge the young person's response to an aspect of the law. It is not that long ago when the young people in the sample were themselves children hampered by the laws and regulations that specifically restrict those under certain ages. For example, the law prohibits the sale of tobacco to children. Today's sixteen to twenty-five year olds are, however, quite in favour of the enforcement of such restrictions: 83.8% consider that it is wrong to sell cigarettes to children under the legal age. They apparently accept that in cases like this the law is right in restricting the freedom of individuals until they come of age to make mature and responsible decisions for themselves.

POLITICS

In the earlier section on values, 46.9% of the sample claim that politics is important to them. The purpose of this section is to explore more deeply what they mean by that. To what extent do sixteen to twenty-five year olds take an active part in politics? To what extent have they made up their minds on key political issues? What in fact are the political attitudes and values which they are espousing? In order to provide indicators to answer these questions, three types of specific items are included in the survey. The first set is concerned with the confidence which the young people place in the party political system through which the country is governed, and the policies of the three major political parties which engage in that system. The second set is concerned with a series of key political issues. The third set is concerned with the politics of wages and the relative social worth of different occupations.

Table 2.8   Politics

	AS%	A%	NC%	D%	DS%
I take an active part in politics	1.6	6.1	13.1	52.3	26.9
It makes no difference which political party is in power	6.5	20.9	22.1	35.4	15.1
I have confidence in the policies of the Labour party	4.3	12.2	39.5	23.5	20.5
I have confidence in the policies of the Conservative party	8.0	18.0	43.4	17.2	13.5
I have confidence in the policies of the Liberal party	0.9	6.8	51.8	24.8	15.7
I think the nationalisation of industry is a good thing	3.5	16.8	38.2	23.7	17.8
I think private schools should be abolished	4.6	7.1	17.0	35.5	35.9
I think private medicine should be abolished	5.8	9.2	19.6	39.0	26.3
I think the trade unions have too much power	32.3	37.3	21.0	7.2	2.2
I think immigration into Britain should be restricted	20.5	40.0	20.6	12.8	6.1
I would rather buy a British car than one made in another country	4.1	11.7	27.8	40.9	15.5
I think the Common Market is a good thing	7.3	36.2	40.4	11.5	4.8
I think too much economic power is in the hands of multinational coporations	11.2	30.5	44.4	12.6	1.3
I think nurses are underpaid for the job they do	36.3	38.4	22.4	2.3	0.6
I think doctors are underpaid for the job they do	22.9	33.5	28.6	12.5	2.6
I think policemen are underpaid for the job they do	16.7	36.1	32.6	10.6	4.0
I think car workers are underpaid for the job they do	1.5	5.0	46.8	30.8	15.9
I think miners are underpaid for the job they do	6.9	18.9	40.8	23.1	10.3
I think clergy are underpaid for the job they do	4.6	17.0	60.5	12.2	5.7

Although 46.9% of the sample claim politics to be of importance to them, very few of them actually take an active part in politics. Only 7.7% agree that they take an active part in politics and of this proportion only 1.6% agree strongly that this is the case. If the young people claim to be interested in politics, their interest is not expressed in active political involvement.

When it comes to an analysis of the English party political system, the young people seem far from certain about which of these parties deserves

31

their confidence. To begin with, one in four is sufficiently doubtful about party politics to claim that it makes no difference which party is in power, and another one in four is not certain whether it makes any difference or not. This means that only two out of every four young people are confident that it does make a difference which party is in power.

Looking at the three major political parties in turn, between one third and one half of the respondents are uncertain whether they have confidence in the policies of these parties or not. 39.5% cannot make up their minds about the Labour party, 43.4% cannot make up their minds about the Conservative party, and 51.8% cannot make up their minds about the Liberal party. On balance, these young people seem to have most confidence in the Conservative party and least confidence in the Liberal party. 26.0% support the Conservatives, 16.5% support the Labour party and 7.7% support the Liberals. This means that half of the young members are the floating voters who do not have consistent confidence in any of the major three parties.

The next batch of questions reviews the attitude of the young people to certain key political issues. Not only do the young people say that they have confidence in the policies of the Conservative party more than they have in the policies of the other parties, they also tend to be conservative in their approach to specific issues. Generally speaking, the young people tend not to be in favour of state control of either industry, education or medicine. The young people seem to be speaking clearly in favour of private enterprise. They speak with more confidence about education and medicine than about industry. 20.0% are in favour of the nationalisation of industry, but just over twice that number (41.5%) are not in favour of it. A very significant proportion (38.2%), however, have not made up their minds. By way of comparison, only 17.0% are uncertain as to whether private schools should be abolished and 19.6% are uncertain about private medicine. 71.4% are clearly in favour of private schools and 65.3% are in favour of private medicine.

The young people are also adopting conservative views on issues as different as the trade unions and immigration. Two out of every three of the sample think that the trade unions have too much power, and one out of every three holds this view strongly. By way of comparison, only one young person in ten disagrees with the notion that the trade unions have too much power, while one in five has not made up his or her mind. Similarly, three out of every five of the sample think that immigration into Britain should be restricted, and one out of every five holds this view strongly. By way of comparison, only one young person in five thinks that immigration should not be restricted, while one in five has not made up his or her mind on this issue. Although such a high proportion of the young people believe that immigration into Britain should be restricted, only a remarkably small proportion are concerned about personally adopting protectionist attitudes towards supporting British industry. Only 15.8% say that they would rather buy a British car than one made in another country, while 56.4% firmly reject this possibility.

The next two questions examine the young person's political attitude towards two aspects of international economics. To begin with, a much greater percentage of the respondents are in favour of the Common Market than are against it. 43.5% think that the Common Market is a good thing, compared with 16.3% who think it is not a good thing. On the other hand, the young people have much less sympathy with the economic and political power wielded by the multinational corporations. Only 13.9% of the respondents consider such power is good, compared with 41.7% who consider it to be bad. It is also important to note how many of the young people, over 40%, have not made up their minds on either of these economic issues.

An interesting way to tap the political values and awareness of people is to select a variety of jobs which have different functions or status in society and to ask the respondents to assess whether the people doing these jobs are being adequately paid for their work or not. The six different employment categories included in the survey are nurses, doctors, policemen, car workers, miners and clergy.

The job which the young people most clearly regarded as being underpaid is that of the nurse. Three out of every four of the respondents think nurses should be paid more. Next, 56.4% regard doctors as being underpaid. Very closely behind doctors come policemen with 52.8% regarding the police as underpaid. The young people appear to place a high value on those working on behalf of society both in health care and in the maintenance of law and order. On the other hand, they have much less concern for those in the industries which they regard as having greater bargaining power in relationship to salary. Only 6.5% think that car workers are underpaid, and 25.8% are concerned that miners are underpaid for the job they do.

The final question of this type focused attention on the clergy. The main impression here is conveyed by the fact that 60.5% of the respondents have no opinion as to whether the clergy are underpaid for the job they do or not. Clergy salaries tend not to be mentioned by the media and clergy themselves have generally neither threatened strike action nor campaigned for salary increases. Young people seem not to have given the question thought, and so they are not in a position to make a judgement.

SOCIETY

What do the young people think about the society in which they live, and to what extent are they concerned about the major issues which affect that society? What are their priorities in relationship to social change, and to what extent are they disturbed by their perceptions of the way in which society is moving?

The first impression to emerge from table 2.9 is that the majority of the young people consider themselves to be living in a declining and decaying society. Around them things seem to be getting worse. To begin with they feel that the world in which they live is becoming less safe. Three out of every four of the respondents are concerned that the crime rate is rising, and the fourth respondent does not really know what to believe about it. Significantly, only 3.9% of the young people do not believe that the crime rate is rising. Looking to the publicly controlled health service and the state system of schools, the young people are convinced that both are in decline. 62.8% believe that the educational standard of schools is declining, and 58.3% believe that the health service is becoming more inefficient. Only a very small minority do not consider this to be the case: 14.2% disagree with this interpretation of the educational system and 13.8% disagree with this interpretation of the health service. In fact, only two out of every five young people are sure that they see a future for Britain at all.

Table 2.9   Society

	AS%	A%	NC%	D%	DS%
I believe that the crime rate is rising	22.5	50.9	22.6	3.6	0.3
I believe that the educational standard of schools is declining	28.4	34.4	22.9	12.1	2.1
I believe that the health service is becoming more inefficient	15.7	42.6	27.9	11.5	2.3
I do not see much future for Britain	5.6	17.7	35.0	30.3	11.4
I believe that the credit card encourages careless spending	12.7	32.4	21.7	26.3	7.0
I believe that it is becoming too easy to obtain an abortion	7.8	16.9	24.8	28.8	21.7
I believe that it is becoming too easy to obtain a divorce	5.9	23.6	26.9	32.2	11.5
I believe that there is too much violence on television	6.4	25.3	25.2	35.3	7.8
I believe that pornography is too readily available	12.6	30.6	25.0	25.0	6.8
I am concerned about the risk of pollution to the environment	34.8	49.9	11.5	3.2	0.7
I am concerned about the rate of inflation	18.0	63.5	12.0	5.8	0.7
I am concerned about people who are homeless	17.5	60.2	15.5	5.6	1.2
I am concerned about the problems of unemployment	16.3	57.2	15.9	8.4	2.2
I am concerned about the risk of nuclear war	31.1	41.6	16.9	9.0	1.5
I am concerned about the poverty of the third world	23.4	45.3	23.3	6.8	1.2

Considerable social changes have taken place during the short space of time covered by the lives of these young people. Three questions were asked to gauge their attitudes towards certain of these changes. The issues chosen were abortion, divorce and credit facilities. Generally, the young people have welcomed the social changes which have come about during the last generation in relationship to divorce and abortion. Only one in four considers that the changes have gone too far and that it is now too easy to obtain a divorce or to obtain an abortion, compared with two out of every four who do not think that society has made it too easy. On the other hand, the young people are not so content with the consequences of living in a credit card society. Although one in three finds no fault with the credit system, 45.1% believe that the credit card encourages careless spending. The young seem happier to live with the greater moral freedom of today's society than with the greater economic freedom.

Two issues of social reform which from time to time receive considerable public attention are the campaign against pornography and the campaign against violence on television. The young people are more concerned about the consequences of pornography than about the consequences of violence on television. Thus, 43.2% believe that pornography is too readily available,

34

compared with 31.7% who believe that there is too much violence on television. Looked at the other way, 31.8% do not believe that pornography is too readily available and 43.1% do not believe that there is too much violence on television. Meanwhile, one young person in four remains to be convinced about either of these issues.

One of the significant features about the responses to the previous nine questions is the high proportion of the young people who check the 'not certain' response. About one in four of the respondents checks this category for each of the questions. This does not indicate a lack of concern with the issues, so much as an unwillingness to make judgements and generalisations about issues regarding which they have insufficient evidence. By way of comparison, the next six questions asked the young members to rate their actual concern about specific issues rather than to make judgements about them. A significantly smaller proportion opt for the neutral response in relationship to these questions.

Generally, the young people demonstrate a considerable degree of concern about the problems which are thought to be major issues confronting today's society. In fact, on average, less than one in ten is uncertain about his or her concern regarding issues like inflation, unemployment, nuclear war, environmental pollution and homelessness. This is another clear indication that the young people consider themselves to be living in uneasy times. While inflation steadily erodes their quality of life, they remain anxious that the very basis of their life is threatened both from within by pollution and form without by nuclear war.

In order of priority, 84.7% are concerned about the risk of pollution to the environment. 81.5% are concerned about the rate of inflation. 77.7% are concerned about people who are homeless. 73.5% are concerned about the problems of unemployment. 72.7% are concerned about the risks of nuclear war. 68.7% are concerned about the poverty of the third world. These percentages demonstrate that the young people are most concerned about the issues that are likely to affect them personally, like the question of pollution, and least concerned about those that are farthest away, like the third world.

Nevertheless, it needs to be stressed that two out of every three of the respondents claim to be concerned about the poverty of the third world. Moreover, the majority of those who do not agree that they are concerned about the third world are motivated by apathy or indifference rather than by hostility to the claims of the third world: 23.3% are uncertain whether they are concerned about this issue or not, compared with only 8.0% who claim to be unconcerned.

WORK

The sections on values and worry have already indicated that the young people take their work seriously: 88.9% claim that their work is important to them, and nearly one in two worry about their work. This section sets out to interpret these statistics within the broader context of the young person's attitude to work. Do they worry about their work because they are unhappy at work, or because they are ambitious to do well? Do they value their work because of the money they earn, or because of the intrinsic job satisfaction?

35

	AS%	A%	NC%	D%	DS%
	Table 2.10	Work			

Table 2.10   Work

	AS%	A%	NC%	D%	DS%
I am happy in my job	24.5	47.2	19.5	6.3	2.5
I like the people I work with	27.5	55.0	13.6	2.6	1.3
I want to get to the top in my work	42.4	37.7	13.5	5.9	0.5
I think it is important to work hard	28.5	58.2	8.2	4.4	0.7
Frequently I wish I could change my job	9.6	16.5	19.1	34.0	20.8
I only work for the money	5.3	11.3	9.5	43.9	30.1
I would rather go on social security than get a job I do not like doing	3.2	14.6	17.5	39.1	25.6

The responses summarised in table 2.10 clearly indicate that the fact that so many young people worry about their work is indicative not of a basic unhappiness at work, but of a genuine ambition to be successful in a competitive environment. Nearly three out of every four (71.7%) are happy in their job, and an even higher proportion (82.5%) like the people they work with. Viewed even more positively, only 8.8% state that they are unhappy in their job and only 3.9% actually dislike the people they work with.

The young person's ambition is clearly indicated by the fact that four in every five of the respondents want to get to the top in their work, and 86.7% think that it is important to work hard. It seems to be ambition rather than unhappiness that prompts 26.1% of the young people to say that they frequently wish that they could change their job, and a further 19.1% to say that they are not certain whether they wish to change their job or not.

Work remains a very important part of the young person's life. It is their work in its own right which the majority of young people value. Their level of job satisfaction is high, and comparatively few of them see work merely as a means to an end. Less than one in six, (16.6%) agree that they only work for the money. Again the importance of work in the lives of these young people is indicated by the fact that two out of every three claim that they would rather have a job they do not like doing than to go on social security.

LEISURE

In today's technological society, leisure time is playing an increasingly important part in the lives of young people. The first objective of this section is to assess how satisfied these young people are with the way in which they spend their leisure time. Table 2.11 indicates that just over half (54.2%) of the young people feel that their leisure time is adequately occupied. Quite a high proportion (35.6%) wish that they had more things to do with their leisure, and the remaining 10.5% are not sure whether they are satisfied with their level of leisure activities or not.

The next four questions assess the relative importance in the lives of the young people of four major leisure activities, namely television, music, reading and social drinking. Music and reading play a much more important part in the lives of the young people than television. While 94.9% often listen to music in their leisure time and 73.1% often read books, only 57.4% report that they watch some television nearly every day. Social drinking is important to half of the respondents: 52.6% of the young people say that they often go drinking with their friends in their leisure time.

Table 2.11   Leisure

	AS%	A%	NC%	D%	DS%
I wish I had more things to do with my leisure time	7.4	27.8	10.5	35.6	18.6
I often read books in my leisure time	27.1	48.0	7.4	13.9	3.5
I often listen to music in my leisure time	46.3	48.6	1.8	3.0	0.2
I watch some television nearly every day	12.2	45.2	5.9	28.3	8.4
I often go drinking with friends in my leisure time	14.9	37.7	8.2	28.9	10.3
I read a newspaper nearly every day	24.2	46.4	9.8	17.1	2.5
I listen to the radio or television news nearly every day	48.2	42.4	3.9	4.7	0.8
I often watch sport in my leisure time	11.0	41.5	12.0	28.3	7.1
I take an active part in sport	27.5	47.1	9.6	13.2	2.6

The majority of these young people use some of their leisure time to keep in touch with what is happening in the world. 70.6% read a newspaper nearly every day and an even higher proportion (90.6%) listen to the radio or television news nearly every day.

Sport plays an important part in the lives of many of the young respondents and their interest is expressed considerably more in terms of participant activity than in terms of a spectator pastime. Thus, 74.6% of the respondents say that they take an active part in sport, compared with 52.5% who say that they often watch sport in their leisure time.

In order to assess the relative interest shown by the respondents in the wide range of leisure pursuits provided by London Central YMCA, the questionnaire listed fifty two of the club's main activities or facilities. Members were asked 'which of the following facilities in London Central YMCA do you use or plan to use?' This simple question makes available a lot of valuable information about the way young people like to spend their leisure time. The swimming pool emerges as the most generally desired facility: 85.7% of the members claim to have an interest in swimming. The coffee bar is the second most popular facility appealing to 71.7% of the members. Next in popularity comes the badminton and squash courts which appeal to 51.7% and 49.8% of the members respectively. The sauna and solarium are also very popular facilities.

Table 2.12   Popularity of Leisure Facilities

Facility	%	Facility	%
Swimming pool	85.7	Martial arts	10.9
Coffee bar	71.7	Swimming classes	10.3
Badminton	51.7	Parachuting classes	10.2
Squash courts	49.8	Chess club	9.3
Sauna	47.1	Judo	9.3
Lounge area	42.6	Painting and drawing class	8.9
Solarium	42.1	Slimnastics courses	8.8
Sports hall	36.6	Craft work shop	8.7
Dance classes	35.3	Do it yourself classes	8.5
Keep fit	35.3	Volley ball club	7.6
Billiards, snooker, pool	33.5	Soccer club	7.6
Film shows	32.8	Slimming class (ladies)	7.2
Table tennis	32.4	Audio studio	7.1
Disco	31.8	Camping equipment	6.1
Weight training	31.1	Climbing equipment	5.3
Tennis	22.0	Handball	5.3
Facials and massage	21.9	Rock climbing	4.6
Reading room	21.6	Kuk sool won classes	4.6
Gymnastics	19.8	Exhibition facilities	4.5
Circuit training	18.4	Mountaineering club	4.1
Basket ball	18.0	Chapel	3.9
Photographic club	16.7	Bridge	3.8
Yoga club	15.0	Cricket club	3.4
Dark room	13.8	Newspaper production	2.9
Trampolining classes	12.6	Bible study	2.9
Sub-aqua club	11.2	Duke of Edinburgh Award	2.4

Over 40.0% of the respondents wish to use the lounge area, and more than 20.0% are interested in using the reading room. The sports hall, dance classes, keep fit and the billiards, snooker and pool facilities also appeal to over a third of the members. Many of the more specialist activities, like volley ball, rock climbing and the bridge club only appeal to a very small minority of the members. One of the great strengths of a club which is able to cater for membership of 7,000 is the way in which a membership of this size enables such a diversity of minority interests to flourish.

COUNSELLING

The final set of questions reviewed from the survey sets out to examine the counselling needs of the young people at the centre of London, together with their perceptions of counselling facilities. It is very apparent that the majority of the young people like living in London. Only 5.8% say that they hate living or working there, and only 10.3% say that they would not advise other young people to come to London to work or to study. The majority remain convinced that London has a lot more to offer the young person than other cities. Nevertheless, the young respondents are well aware that the city has its disadvantages and dangers. Indeed, a third of the respondents (34.7%) consider that the young person has to cope with more risks in London than in other cities, while 25.8% of the respondents think that it is all too easy to get mixed up with prostitution in a place like London, while even more (35.6%) think that it is all too easy to get mixed up with drugs. Consequently, there is general agreement among the young people that there should be more counselling facilities for young people in London. 62.7% agree that this should be a priority, compared with 4.2% who disagree that there is a need for an expansion of such facilities. The other 33.1% are not sure.

Table 2.13   Counselling

	AS%	A%	NC%	D%	DS%
I hate London	1.5	4.3	12.4	45.7	36.2
The young person has to cope with more risks in London than in other cities	8.4	26.3	24.7	30.7	9.9
I think it is all too easy to get mixed up with prostitution in a place like London	5.0	20.8	26.8	34.4	12.9
I think it is all too easy to get mixed up with drugs in a place like London	7.3	28.3	21.5	31.6	11.3
I think that London has a lot more to offer the young person than other cities	13.6	42.0	29.6	12.3	2.4
I would not advise a young person to come to London to work or to study	2.8	7.5	21.9	44.9	22.9
I think there should be more counselling faciliti es for young people in London	15.3	47.4	33.1	3.3	0.9
From time to time I feel I need to talk my problems over with someone	14.9	60.9	8.2	13.5	2.5
I have found it helpful to talk about my problems with close friends	30.6	46.0	10.5	10.5	2.3
I have found it helpful to talk about my problems with my mother	20.5	39.6	14.3	20.8	4.8
I have found it helpful to talk about my problems with my father	8.4	27.4	15.2	30.6	18.4
I have found it helpful to talk about my problems with a minister of religion	2.6	9.1	27.4	41.6	19.3
I have found it helpful to talk about my problems with a trained counsellor	1.6	9.7	28.0	41.4	19.3
I would never discuss my problems with a trained counsellor	6.6	14.4	36.1	32.2	10.8
I would never discuss my problems with a minister of religion	10.7	24.2	35.6	24.6	4.9

Three quarters of the sixteen to twenty-five year olds who responded to the questionnaire say that from time to time they need to talk over their problems with someone. Looking back over their past experience of talking about their problems with others, 60.1% report that they have found it helpful to talk with their mother, while 35.8% report that they have found it helpful to talk with their father. A greater source of help has been derived from discussion with close friends. Three out of four of the young people (76.6%) have found close friends helpful in this kind of way. By way of contrast, comparatively few of the young people have ever derived help from talking about their problems with professionals. Only just over 11.0% of the respondents say that they have been helped by either a counsellor or a minister of religion.

When asked to speculate about the people to whom they might turn for advice in the future, over a third of the young people had not made up their minds whether they would be willing to talk with a minister of religion or a trained counsellor. Those who have made up their minds on this issue are considerably less reluctant to turn to a counsellor than to a minister of religion. Thus, 34.9% of the respondents said that they would never discuss their problems with a minister of religion, compared with 21.0% who said that they would never discuss their problems with a trained counsellor. There is certainly a marked reluctance on the part of some young people to turn to professionals for help, and the barrier is much stronger in the case of the clergy than in the case of the counsellor.

NOTES

[1]   See for example Peter Warr, 'A study of psychological well-being', British Journal of Psychology, 69, 111 - 121, 1978.
[2]   See for example D. O'Donovan, 'An historical review of the lie scale with particular reference to Maudsley Personality Inventory', Papers in Psychology, 3, 13 - 19, 1969; S.B.G. Eysenck, D.K.B. Nias, and H.J. Eysenck,'Interpretation of the Children's lie scale scores', British Journal of Educational Psychology, 41, 23 - 31, 1971.
[3]   On this interpretation of the lie scale see for example T.G. Crookes and S.J. Buckley, 'Lie score and insight', Irish Journal of Psychology, 3, 134 - 6, 1976.

3 Men and Women

In this chapter, the responses to the questionnaire are analysed and
explored in terms of the differences between men and women within the
twelve key areas of well-being, worry, values, self image, beliefs, morals,
law, politics, society, work, leisure and counselling. These differences
make a fascinating study in gender differentiation.

WELL-BEING

There are not many major differences between the sexes in terms of
positive well-being in the inner city. Basically the same high proportion
of men and women find their lives really worth living (84%) and feel that
their lives have a sense of purpose (73%).

However, at the other end of the continuum of well-being, the women in
the sample report significantly more signs of stress than the men. More
of the women say that they often feel depressed than the men, and more
of the women are worried that they cannot cope. More women than men
say that they have at some time or other considered taking their own lives.
The women both feel the need for more company by linking to have lots of
people around them, and at the same time they more often say that they
find crowds oppressive.

Table 3.1   Well-being

	Men %	Women %
I like to have a lot of people around me	53	66
I find crowds oppressive	32	48
I often feel depressed	26	32
I am worried that I cannot cope	11	16
I have sometimes considered taking my own life	17	22

It is the men, however, who report a greater feeling of isolation in the
city. 25% of the men say that they tend to be lonely compared with 19%
of the women, and 17% of the men feel that no one knows them compared
with 12% of the women. It is, however, the women who more often feel
the need for someone to turn to for support. Thus, 28% of the women say
that they often long for someone to turn to for advice, compared with 23%

41

of the men. Similarly, 52% of the women say that they long for someone
to turn to for affection, compared with 47% of the men.

WORRY

In a number of ways, life in the inner city seems to be causing the same
levels of worry among both men and women. 46% of the men are concerned
about their work, and so are 46% of the women. 22% of the men are
worried about their debts, and so are 23% of the women. 66% of the men
are worried about the world situation, and so are 63% of the women. Both
the men and the women seem to be responding to these pressures in the
same kind of way. 10% of the men are worried that they might have a
breakdown, and so are 9% of the women.

Table 3.2   Worry

	Men %	Women %
I am worried about my relationships with other people	25	20
I am worried about my sex life	18	12
I am worried about my health	29	19
I am worried about growing old	23	31
I am worried I might get cancer	28	39

Where the differences in levels of worry occur between the sexes are
in the areas of personal relationships and health. The men tend to worry
about their relationships with other people more than the women, and the
men also say that they are more worried about their sex lives. Generally,
the men are more worried about their health than the women. However,
it is the women who are considerably more worried that they might get
cancer. It is the women too, who are more worried about growing old.

VALUES

There are some interesting similarities as well as some important
differences in the values of the young men and women. Both the men
and the women attach the same high importance to their work, their
friends, their family and their home. The men and the women both
attribute the same low importance to religion. On the other hand, the
men consider politics more important than the women, while the women
consider moral values more important than the men.

The women have a different set of economic values from those held by
the men. On the one hand, the men are more concerned with making
money than the women. On the other hand, the women are more concerned
with saving money than the men. Both men and women attach the same
importance to spending money. Although the women are more concerned
with saving money, it is the men who find it more important to look to
the future in terms of owning their own home. 77% of the men say that
it is important for them to own their own home compared with 71% of
the women. Similarly, the men and women have a different set of

personal values. The women attribute greater importance both to their appearance and to what people think of them. 93% of the women say that their appearance is important to them, compared with 86% of the men. 76% of the women agree that what people think of them is important, compared with 67% of the men. The men adopt a significantly more hedonistic approach to life. 8% more of the men than of the women consider having a good time is more important than anything else.

Table 3.3   Values

	Men %	Women %
Making money is important to me	69	63
Saving money is important to me	68	75
Moral values are important to me	78	84
Politics is important to me	49	35
Having a good time is more important than anything else	36	28

SELF IMAGE

In a number of ways the men and the women share the same concept of self image and social desirability. The same proportion of men and women agree that they have told lies, broken their promises and taken advantage of people. The same high proportion of men and women also say that they are always willing to admit when they have made a mistake.

However, there are differences in self image between the sexes in the areas of jealousy, resentment and theft. More of the men admit to having stolen something in the course of their lives. More of the women admit to feelings of resentment when they do not get their own way. More of the women also admit to feelings of jealousy.

Table 3.4   Self Image

	Men %	Women %
Sometimes I have been jealous of others	72	84
Sometimes I feel resentful when I do not get my own way	60	68
I have never stolen anything in my life	23	40
Sometimes I have taken advantage of people	60	59

BELIEFS

Although the same proportion of men and women claim that religion is important to them, this section clearly demonstrates that the women are considerably more religious than the men in terms of their beliefs, attitudes and practices. To begin with more women than men claim to believe in God. Similarly only 10% of the women claim to be atheists, compared with 17% of the men. Almost the same proportion of men and women claim to be agnostics. In response to another question, 67% of the men say that they are not practising members of any religious group compared with 61% of the women.

Table 3.5   Beliefs

	Men %	Women %
I believe in God	54	62
I believe that Jesus Christ is the Son of God	41	50
I think religious education should be taught in schools	53	65
The church seems irrelevant for life today	29	16
I believe in life after death	39	48

In terms of their assent to the proposition 'I believe that Jesus Christ is the Son of God', 41% of the men would be regarded as Christians compared with 50% of the women. In terms of affiliation to a Christian denomination, 22% of the men and 33% of the women say that they are members of a church. The most striking difference in denominational affiliation concerns the Church of England. 18% of the women claim to be Church of England, compared with only 8% of the men. 10% of the men and 12% of the women are Roman Catholic. 4% of the men and 3% of the women belong to other Christian denominations. 10% of the men and 5% of the women claim to be active members of other world faiths.

In spite of the fact that more women than men claim to be practising members of a religious group, the same proportion of both sexes, about 6%, agree that they take an active part in a church. These responses seem to be confirmed by an analysis of the difference in church attendance among men and women. There is little difference in terms of those who attended church within the last month, but significantly more women are casual attenders who have been to church within the last year. Thus 58% of the women say that they have been to a place of worship at least once within the past year, compared with 51% of the men. Similarly, although there is little difference between male and female in terms of those who have recently read the Bible, many more women than men have recently prayed. 71% of the women say that they have prayed within the last year, compared with 50% of the men. 30% of the men and 32% of the women have read the Bible within the last year.

The men are more inclined than the women to reject the relevance both of the Bible and the church. 27% of the men agree that the Bible seems irrelevant for life today, compared with 19% of the women. Similarly, 30% of the men agree that the church seems irrelevant for life today compared with 16% of the women. More women than men think that religious education should be taught in schools.

The greater tendency of women to accept religious beliefs is not confined to their acceptance of Christian beliefs. For example, significantly more women than men accept the Christian belief of life after death. At the same time, more women than men also believe in reincarnation. 28% of the

44

women believe in reincarnation, compared with 21% of the men.

Moving away from the religious sphere to other areas of belief, it is interesting to note that women tend more than men both to believe in their horoscopes and to believe that luck plays an important part in their lives. Thus, 23% of the women believe in their horoscope, compared with 14% of the men, while only 23% of the women are convinced that luck plays no part in their lives , compared with 28% of the men.

MORALS

The men and women in the sample hold almost identical attitudes to the issues of drugs and alcohol. 33% of the men and 31% of the women believe that it is wrong to become drink. 79% of the men and 80% of the women believe that it is wrong to use heroin. 40% of the men and 36% of the women believe that it is wrong to use marijuana. The men and women also hold very similar views on the issue of heterosexual ethics. 11% of the men and 9% of the women think it is wrong to have sexual intercourse outside marriage. 7% of the men and 4% of the women say that it is wrong for an unmarried couple to live together. Where there are clear differences between the sexes in their moral attitudes are in the areas of war, euthanasia, abortion and contraception. On the one hand, the women are more opposed to war than men. On the other hand, the women are more accepting than the men of euthanasia. The men are less certain than the women about the ethics of both abortion and contraception. 94% of the women clearly disagree with the notion that contraception is wrong, compared with 84% of the men. 12% of the men say that they are uncertain about their views on contraception, compared with only 4% of the women. Similarly, 74% of the women clearly disagree with the notion that abortion is wrong, compared with 65% of the men.

Table 3.6   Morals

	Men %	Women %
I think all war is wrong	58	66
I think abortion is wrong	17	11
I think euthanasia is wrong	26	20
I think it is wrong to have sexual intercourse outside marriage	11	9
I think the practice of homosexuality is wrong	34	12

The largest difference in the area of moral attitudes between men and women concerns their understanding of homosexuality. Men are much less accepting of homosexuality than women. 71% of the women disagree that homosexuality is wrong compared with 47% of the men.

LAW

In response to each of the questions about obedience to the law, the women either hold the same view as the men or a stricter view. In no case do the women adopt a more lenient view than the men. The same proportion of men and women agree that tax returns should be filled in with complete honesty. Similarly, the same proportion of men and women argue that it is wrong to travel without a ticket even if you are not caught. However, 6% more women than men say that it is wrong to bring an extra bottle of spirits through the customs, and 9% more women say that it is wrong to sell cigarettes to children under the legal age.

Table 3.7   Law

	Men %	Women %
I disagree with selling cigarettes to children under the legal age	80	89
There is nothing wrong in bringing an extra bottle of spirits through the customs if you are not caught	46	40
I think speed limits should be strictly obeyed	57	68
I disagree with drinking and driving	86	93

On the issue of the law and the motorist, the same proportion (46%) of both men and women agree that parking restrictions should be strictly obeyed. 11% more women than men say that speed limits should be strictly obeyed and 6% more women than men disagree that there is nothing wrong with drinking and driving.

POLITICS

Generally, the women in the sample tend to be more conservative in their political views than the men. 30% of the women say that they have confidence in the policies of the Conservative party, compared with 23% of the men. 12% of the women say that they have confidence in the policies of the Labour party compared with 20% of the men. By way of comparison, the same proportion of men and women, about 8% have confidence in the policies of the Liberal party.

The men and women in the sample are both inactive politically speaking, only 9% of the men and 6% of the women say that they take an active part in politics. Both sexes are equally sceptical about politics. 29% of the men and 25% of the women say that it makes no difference which political party is in power.

On the industrial front, women are less in favour of both nationalisation and trade unions than the men. 74% of the women think that the trade unions have too much power, compared with 66% of the men. 16% of the women think that the nationalisation of industry is a good thing, compared with 23% of the men. Similarly, the women are less in favour of the abolition of private schools and private medicine.

The women tend to adopt a more protectionist view towards their country when they are invited to decide on the issue of immigration and a less protectionist view when they are invited to decide on the issue of supporting home industry. Thus, more women than men think that immigration into Britain should be restricted, while less women than men say they would wish to support British industry by preferring to buy a British car than one made in another country.

Table 3.8   Politics

	Men %	Women %
I think immigration into Britain should be restricted	55	67
I would rather buy a British car than one made in another country	18	12
I think private schools should be abolished	15	8
I think private medicine should be abolished	18	11
I think clergy are underpaid for the job they do	19	25
I think nurses are underpaid for the job they do	70	81

Men are more in favour of the Common Market than women. 47% of the men think that the Common Market is a good thing, compared with 39% of the women. The same proportion of men and women think that too much economic power is in the hands of multinational corporations.

There is a clear tendency for women to be more sympathetic towards the pay claims of the helping professions than men. 11% more of the women think that nurses are underpaid for the job they do, and 59% of the women think that doctors are underpaid, compared with 54% of the men. Similarly, 56% of the women think that policemen are underpaid for the job they do compared with 51% of the men. 6% more of the women think that the clergy are underpaid. There are no differences between the men and the women in their evaluation of miners and car workers.

SOCIETY

In respect of ten of the fifteen issues of social concern reviewed by the survey, there were no significant differences in the levels of concern shown by the men and by the women. For example, 73% of the men and 74% of the women believe that the crime rate is rising, 59% of the men and 57% of the women believe that the health service is becoming more inefficient, and 45% of the men and 45% of the women believe that the credit card encourages careless spending. The men and women hold similarly close levels of concern about the poverty of the third world, the risk of nuclear war, homelessness, pollution, divorce, inflation and the future of Britain.

Regarding four of the five issues where there is a significant difference in the concern shown by men and women, the women show a higher level of concern than the men. More women believe that the educational standard of schools is declining. More women believe that pornography is too readily available, and that there is too much violence on television. More women are concerned about the problems of unemployment. On the other hand, more men than women believe that it is becoming too easy to obtain an abortion.

47

Table 3.9   Society

	Men %	Women %
I believe that the educational standard of schools is declining	58	69
I believe that there is too much violence on television	24	41
I believe that pornography is too readily available	37	51
I am concerned about the problems of unemployment	69	79
I believe that it is becoming too easy to obtain an abortion	27	21

WORK

There are some significant differences in the work experience profiles of the men and women in the sample. A greater proportion of the male members are students, 37% compared with 21% of the women. A greater proportion of the female members have experienced unemployment during the past two years, 37% compared with 27% of the men. The average take home pay of the female members is about £52 a week, five pounds less than the average £57 taken home by the male members. These averages, however, conceal the fact that the distribution of income is more widely spread for the men. On the one hand, 6% more men than women receive less than £40 per week. On the other hand, 12% more men than women receive over £80 per week.

Basically, the same proportion of men and women enjoy their work. 74% of the women and 70% of the men say that they are happy in their job. 80% of the men and 84% of the women agree that they like the people they work with. 24% of the men and 28% of the women say that they frequently wish they could change their job.

Table 3.10   Work

	Men %	Women %
I think it is important to work hard	84	90
I only work for the money	21	11
I want to get to the top in my work	83	76
I would rather go on social security than get a job I do not like doing	20	14

However, the men and the women do hold some quite different values associated with their work. The women seem to find greater intrinsic satisfaction from their work. More women agree that it is important to work hard and fewer say that they only work for the money. Similarly, more of the women are clear that they would not rather go on social security than get a job they do not like doing. On the other hand, it is the men who are more ambitious than the women about their work. More men say that they want to get to the top in their work.

LEISURE

More men than women are dissatisfied with the way in which they spend their leisure time. 38% of the men compared with 32% of the women wish that they had more things to do with their leisure.

Men and women share the same level of interest in listening to music, watching television and reading the newspaper. Where their levels of interest do differ are in relationship to books and sport. The women are much more interested in reading books. The men are more interested in sport, both as spectators and as participants.

Table 3.11   Leisure

	Men %	Women %
I wish I had more things to do with my leisure time	38	32
I often read books in my leisure time	68	84
I take an active part in sport	78	70
I often watch sport in my leisure time	58	46

As it is to be expected, some of the leisure facilities and activities provided by London Central YMCA appeal equally to men and to women, while some are more popular among the women and others are more popular among the men. The facilities and activities which appeal equally to both sexes are, in alphabetical order, badminton, Bible study, bridge, camping equipment, chapel, climbing equipment, disco, do-it-yourself, Duke of Edinburgh Award, exhibition facilities, gymnastics, hand ball, mountain-eering club, newspaper production, rock climbing, squash courts, sub-aqua club, swimming pool, swimming classes, tennis and volley ball club.

The facilities more frequently chosen by the women tend to be orientated towards health and beauty, like keep fit, facials and massage, slimnastics courses, the sauna and the solarium, or towards craft activities, like the craft work shop and the painting and drawing classes. The women also make more use of the social facilities, like the lounge and coffee bar.

The facilities most frequently chosen by the men tend to be orientated towards the most strenuous activities, like weight training, parachuting and the martial arts, or towards the traditional male sports, like cricket, soccer and billiards. The men also make more use of the technical facilities, like the dark room and audio studio, and show a greater interest in film shows and the reading room. Also the chess club and table tennis are both preferred more by men than by women.

Table 3.12   Leisure Facilities

	Men %	Women %
Facilities preferred by women		
Coffee bar	69	76
Craft work shop	5	13
Dance classes	15	62
Facials and massage	10	38
Keep fit	30	42
Lounge area	40	47
Painting and drawing classes	5	13
Sauna	41	55
Slimnastics courses	2	17
Slimming classes	0	16
Solarium	34	53
Trampolining classes	6	21
Yoga classes	7	25
Facilities preferred by men		
Audio studio	9	4
Basket ball	24	9
Billiards, snooker, pool	50	11
Chess club	14	3
Circuit training	28	5
Cricket club	1	0
Dark room	16	10
Film shows	35	30
Judo	13	5
Kuk sool won classes	7	2
Martial arts	16	4
Parachuting courses	13	6
Photographic club	19	13
Reading room	24	19
Soccer club	12	2
Sports hall	44	27
Table tennis	39	23
Weight training	50	6

COUNSELLING

There is an equal concern among both the young men and the young women regarding the need for counselling facilities in central London. 63% of the men and 62% of the women say that there should be more counselling facilities for young people in London.

Underlying this very close agreement, the men and women have significantly different perceptions of the impact of London on young people. More men tend to believe both that London has more to offer the young person and at the same time that London presents more risks for the young person. 59% of the men think that London has a lot more to offer the young person than other cities, compared with 51% of the women. At the same time 38% of the men believe that the young person has to cope with more risks in London than in other cities, compared with 30%

of the women. 12% of the men say that they would not advise a young person to come to London to work or to study, compared with 7% of the women.

Table 3.13   Counselling

	Men %	Women %
I think that London has a lot more to offer the young person than other cities	59	52
The young person has to cope with more risks in London than in other cities	30	38
From time to time I feel I need to talk my problems over with someone	68	87
I would never discuss my problems with a minister of religion	36	33
I would never discuss my problems with a trained counsellor	24	17

Considerably more of the women say that from time to time they feel the need to talk their problems over with someone. This need is reflected in the fact that 85% of the women say that they have found it helpful to talk about their problems with close friends, compared with 70% of the men. Similarly, a larger proportion (67%) of the women have found it helpful to talk about their problems with their mother, compared with 55% of the men. There is, however, no significant difference between the proportions of the men and women who have found it helpful to talk about their problems with their father.

Although more women than men say that they need to discuss their problems with someone, the women have not had more experience of gaining help from trained counsellors or ministers of religion. 9% of the women and 13% of the men say that they have found it helpful to talk about their problems with a trained counsellor. 10% of the women and 13% of the men have found it helpful to talk about their problems with a minister of religion. Looking to the future, the men and women appear to be equally reluctant to discuss their problems with a minister of religion. However, the women are significantly less reluctant than the men to consider discussing their problems with a trained counsellor.

4 Teens and Twenties

In order to examine the relationship between age and the attitudes of the young people, comparisons were made between two groups, the sixteen to twenty-one year old and the twenty-two to twenty-five year old. These two age bands will be referred to in the following discussion as the late teenage and the early twenties groups respectively.

WELL-BEING

The over twenty-ones are slightly more secure in themselves than the younger members, and they enjoy a slightly greater degree of psychological well-being. However, differences are not in fact all that great, and at some points the early twenties group seems to be less happy in the inner city than the late teenage group. For example, although the same proportion of the older and younger group say that they find life really worth living, more of the early twenties group have come to sense a purposelessness in their lives. 9% of the early twenties group say that they do not feel their life has a sense of purpose compared with only 4% of the late teenage group.

Table 4.1   Well-being

	16-21 %	22-25 %
I like to have a lot of people around me	61	56
I find crowds oppressive	34	44
I often feel depressed	32	25
I have sometimes considered taking my own life	22	16

The early twenties group finds city life slightly less congenial than the late teenage group. 56% of the older group say that they like to have a lot of people around them, compared with 61% of the younger group. Similarly, 10% more of the early twenties group say that they find crowds oppressive.

Basically, the same proportions of the late teenage and early twenties groups experience isolation in the inner city and long for someone to turn to from time to time. 23% of the older group and 21% of the younger group say they tend to be lonely. 14% of the older group and 15% of the

52

younger group feel that no one knows them. 49% of the older group and 50% of the younger group often long for someone to turn to for affection. 24% of the older group and 26% of the younger group often long for someone to turn to for advice.

Although in a number of ways the early twenties group is experiencing the same pressures as the late teenage group, and in fact feels more oppressed by the crowds in the inner city, the older group has learnt to deal with these pressures more effectively. 7% less of the early twenties group say that they often feel depressed. 78% of the older group say that they are not worried about their ability to cope, compared with 70% of the younger group. Finally, 6% less of the older group say that sometimes they have considered taking their own lives.

WORRY

There are very few significant differences in the levels of worry exhibited by the late teenage and the early twenties groups. The same proportions of both groups are worried about the world situation, their work, their debts, their relationships and their sex lives. Interestingly, the older group is no more worried than the younger group about growing old. 26% of the older group are worried about growing old, and so are 27% of the younger group.

Table 4.2   Worry

	16–21 %	22–25 %
I am worried about my sex life	16	16
I am worried about growing old	27	26
I am worried about my health	27	22
I am worried I might get cancer	30	36

Where the two age groups do differ in their levels of worry is in relationship to the issue of health. Generally, young people in their early twenties worry less about their health than those in their late teens, but at the same time they worry more about the specific problem of cancer. 5% fewer members of the older age group say that they worry about their health, but 6% more of the older age group say that they are worried that they might get cancer. Regarding their mental health, 11% of the younger age group say they are worried they might have a breakdown, compared with 9% of the older age group.

VALUES

While the value attributed to a number of areas remains the same among both the late teenage and the early twenties groups, there are also some interesting differences between the two separate age groups. To begin with there are some interesting differences as well as some interesting similarities in the economic values of the two groups. Although the younger and older groups attach the same importance both to making money and to spending money, a significant difference exists in their attitude towards saving money. 68% of the early twenties group think that saving money is important, compared with 74% of the late teenage group. The older age group does not, however, show any less interest in looking to the future in terms of the ownership of property. 74% of the older group think that it is important for them to own their own house, compared with 73% of the younger group.

Table 4.3   Values

	16–21 %	22–25 %
Religion is important to me	35	28
Politics is important to me	42	52
Moral values are important to me	77	84
Having a good time is more important than anything else	36	29

Both age groups attach the same importance to their appearance, their friends, their work, their home and their family. For example, 89% of both age groups say that their appearance is important to them and 95% of both age groups say that their friends are important to them. Both age groups are equally concerned regarding what other people think of them. 72% of the older group and 70% of the younger group agree that what people think of them is important.

There is an important relationship between age and the value ascribed to religion, morals and politics. On the one hand, there is a significant decline in the area of religion. 7% less of the older group consider that religion is important to them. On the other hand, there is a significant increase in the areas of politics and morals. 10% more of the older group say that politics is important to them, and 7% more of the older group say that moral values are important to them. The increased acceptance of moral responsibility which comes with age is indicated by the decline of 7% in those who agree that having a good time is more important than anything else.

SELF IMAGE

Age has very little relationship with most of the aspects of self image. The same proportion of the early twenties group and the late teenage group admit to telling lies, breaking promises, stealing and feeling resentment when they do not get their own way. The same proportion of both age groups say that they are always willing to admit when they make a mistake. On the other hand, the young people in their early twenties are more likely than those in their late teens to report both that they experience feelings of jealousy, and that they have taken advantage of people. Thus 80% of the early twenties group say that they sometimes have been jealous of others compared with 74% of the late teens group. 64% of the early twenties group say that sometimes they have taken advantage of people, compared with 56% of the late teens group.

BELIEFS

The early twenties group reports a significantly lower commitment to both religious beliefs and religious practices than the late teens group. Roughly the same proportion, between 28% and 29%, of the younger and older groups would claim to be agnostic, but in the early twenties group there are both a significant increase in the number of atheists and a significant decrease in the number of theists. Thus 17% of the young people in their early twenties claim that they do not believe in God, compared with 11% of those in their late teens.

The same proportion (27%) of both the younger and the older groups claim to belong to a Christian denomination. Of these, only 6% of both age groups claim to take an active part in a church. Although the nominal allegiance to a Christian denomination remains the same within the two age groups, 6% less of the older group claim to believe that Jesus Christ is the Son of God.

Table 4.4   Beliefs

	16–21 %	22–25 %
I believe in my horoscope	22	14
I believe in reincarnation	28	20
I believe in life after death	48	38
I believe that Jesus Christ is the Son of God	48	42
I believe in God	61	54

Close inspection of the reported religious behaviour of the older group shows that they pray less often, read the Bible less often and attend a place of worship less often than the younger group. The significant point is that those in the older age group stand much further away from their most recent contact with religious practice. Whereas 36% of the younger group read the Bible within the last year, only 23% of the older group did so. Whereas 66% of the younger group had prayed within the last year, only 57% of the older age group did so. Only 51% of the older group attended a place of worship within the last year, compared with 57% of the younger group.

Differences in church attendance and Bible reading are not reflected in a difference in attitude towards the relevance of either the church or the Bible. The same proportion of both age groups, about one quarter, say that the church and the Bible are irrelevant for life today. Similarly, 58% of both age groups think that religious education should be taught in schools. These statistics seem to indicate that the church is losing the allegiance of the young much faster than it is losing their goodwill.

The twenty-two to twenty-five year age group of young people are less certain about the supernatural side of life in general. 10% less believe in life after death and 8% less believe in reincarnation. This loss of faith is not restricted simply to the religious area. 8% less of those in their early twenties believe in their horoscope compared with those in their late teens. On the other hand the same proportion of both age groups continue to believe that there is intelligent life on other planets, and that luck plays an important part in their lives.

MORALS

Age brings about a number of revisions in moral attitudes. Where revision takes place, the tendency is towards greater liberalism, but also towards greater moral responsibility. The continued movement of the young away from the traditional moral absolutes is not to be understood as an expression of moral irresponsibility. The nature of this transition is neatly illustrated by comparing the changes that take place in the young person's attitude towards alcohol, marijuana and heroin. While there is a greater acceptance of both drunkenness and the use of marijuana, there is an increased rejection of the use of the more dangerous drug heroin.

The late teenage group has already adopted a very liberal attitude towards heterosexual ethics. There is little room for further liberalisation to take place with age. Only a very small minority of both the late teenage and the early twenties groups think that either contraception or extra-marital intercourse are wrong. 3% of both age groups says that contraception is wrong. 11% of the younger group and 9% of the older group think that it is wrong to have sexual intercourse outside marriage. 7% of the older group and 5% of the younger group think that it is wrong for an unmarried couple to live together.

Table 4.5   Morals

	16–21 %	22–25 %
I think it is wrong to become drunk	34	29
I think it is wrong to use marijuana	43	33
I think it is wrong to use heroin	75	83
I think the practice of homosexuality is wrong	29	20

Where there is a significant difference with age in attitude towards a matter of sexual ethics is in relationship to the issue of homosexuality. The early twenties group is significantly more accepting of homosexuality than the late teenage group. Nevertheless both the late teenage and the early twenties groups remain less liberal in their attitude towards homosexual ethics than towards heterosexual ethics.

No significant differences in attitude occur with age in relationship to the issues of war, euthanasia or abortion. Attitudes formed on these issues during the late teens appear to remain stable into the early twenties. 14% of both groups think that abortion is wrong. 25% of the older group and 22% of the younger group think that euthanasia is wrong. 61% of both age groups think all war is wrong.

LAW

As the young people grow older, so they tend to adopt more law abiding attitudes. 9% less of the early twenties group are willing to condone travelling without a ticket. 6% more of the early twenties group consider that tax returns should be filled in with complete honesty. Similarly, 41% of the older group think that it is wrong to bring an extra bottle of spirits through the customs, compared with 36% of the younger group. 86% of the older group think that it is wrong to sell cigarettes to children under the legal age, compared with 82% of the younger group.

Table 4.6   Law

	16-21 %	22-25 %
It is not wrong to travel without a ticket if you are not caught	25	16
I think tax returns should be filled in with complete honesty	50	56
I disagree with drinking and driving	86	92
I think speed limits should be strictly obeyed	61	62

Although already 86% of the younger group disagree that there is nothing wrong with drinking and driving, even a larger proportion of the older group agree that the law should be upheld on this point. Roughly the same proportions of both age groups think that parking restrictions and speed limits should be strictly obeyed.

POLITICS

There are very few differences in political attitudes between the sixteen to twenty-one and the twenty-two to twenty-five year age groups. The political attitudes formed during late adolescence appear to be carried through to young adulthood. There is a marginal increase in interest shown in politics and the allegiance given to each of the major political parties by the older group, but this difference is very small. 7% of the younger and 9% of the older groups say that they take an active part in politics. 14% of the younger and 18% of the older groups say that they have confidence in the policies of the Labour party. 7% of the younger and 9% of the older groups have confidence in the policies of the Liberal party. 25% of the younger and 26% of the older groups have confidence in the policies of the Conservative party. This means than an extra 7% of the older group seem committed to one of the major political parties. In spite of this increase in apparent party affiliation, the same proportions (27%) of both age groups remain sceptical about the whole system of party politics and say that it makes no difference which political party is in power.

Both the younger and the older members tend to be equally conservative in their approach to specific political issues. Only 21% of the younger and 20% of the older groups think that the nationalisation of industry is a good thing. 11% of the younger and 12% of the older groups think that private schools should be abolished. 14% of the younger and 16% of the older groups think that private medicine should be abolished. 69% of the younger and 70% of the older groups think that the trade unions have too much power. 60% of the younger and 61% of the older groups think that immigration into Britain should be restricted.

The closeness of the attitudes held by young people in their late teens and those in their early twenties in relationship to so many issues of national politics makes even more noticeable the differences in their views regarding international issues. 44% of the older group consider that there is too much economic power in the hands of multinational corporations, compared with 39% of the younger group. 17% more of the older group consider that the Common Market is a good thing.

Table 4.7   Politics

	16-21 %	22-25 %
I think the Common Market is a good thing	35	52
I think too much economic power is in the hands of multinational corporations	39	44
I think clergy are underpaid for the job they do	18	25
I think nurses are underpaid for the job they do	72	78

The older group is significantly more sympathetic to the pay conditions of both nurses and clergy. The latter is surprising, given the increased alienation of the older group from religion in general. On the other hand, there are no differences between the two groups' evaluation of doctors, policemen, carworkers or miners.

SOCIETY

The young person's perception of the condition of British society does not seem to undergo many changes with age. The sense of living in a declining society persists throughout the age range of sixteen to twenty-five years. 73% of the young people in their late teens and 74% of those in their early twenties believe that the crime rate is rising. 23% of both age groups say that they do not see much future for Britain. 63% of both age groups believe that the educational standard of schools is declining. Where there is a heightened sense of crisis in in relationship to the health service. 62% of the older group are convinced that the health service is becoming more inefficient, compared with 55% of the younger group.

The young person's attitude to the moral climate of Britain seems to become more accepting with age. Whereas 47% of the younger group believe that pornography is too readily available, only 39% of the older group believe this to be the case. Whereas 33% of the younger group believe that it is becoming too easy to obtain a divorce, only 26% of the older group believe this to be the case. Similarly, 56% of the older group disagree that it is becoming too easy to obtain an abortion, compared with 45% of the younger group; and 37% of the older group deny that the credit card encourages careless spending, compared with

29% of the younger group.

Table 4.8   Society

	16–21 %	22–25 %
I am concerned about the rate of inflation	78	85
I am concerned about the people who are homeless	74	81
I am concerned about the risk of nuclear war	70	75
I am concerned about the poverty of the third world	65	73

The general trend towards increased acceptance of the social trends regarding pornography, abortion and divorce, makes the direction of difference in attitude towards the level of violence on television even more noticeable. In fact, 35% of the older group believe that there is too much violence on television, compared with 28% of the younger group.

The young person's professed concern about the issues of social importance in the 1980's increases in relationship to all of the six issues covered by the survey. 8% more of the older group are concerned about the poverty of the third world. 7% more are concerned about the problems of inflation and homelessness. 5% more are concerned about the risk of nuclear war, pollution to the environment and unemployment. 87% of the older group are concerned about the risk of pollution to the environment, compared with 82% of the younger group. 76% of the older group are concerned about the problems of unemployment, compared with 71% of the younger group.

WORK

There are some very obvious relationships between age and the work experience of the members. 41% of the sixteen to twenty-one year age group are students, compared with 17% of the twenty-two to twenty-five year age group. Of those who are not students of both age groups, considerably more of the older group have attained jobs in the professional or semi-professional spheres. Similarly, there is a considerable difference in the average take home pay or weekly income (including student grants) of the two age groups. The young people in their late teens average £47.00 per week, while those in their early twenties average £62.00 per week after all deductions have been taken into consideration. A large proportion of both groups, 29% of the older and 34% of the younger, have experienced some unemployment during the past two years.

Both age groups attach considerable importance to their work. 87% of the younger and 90% of the older groups say that their work is important to them. 87% of the older and 86% of the younger groups think that it is important to work hard. Similarly, both groups seem to derive considerable satisfaction from their work. 72% of both groups say that they are happy in their job. 82% of the younger and 83% of the older groups say that they like the people they work with. Only 18% of the younger and 15% of the older groups consider that they only work for the money.

However, there are also a few significant differences in the young person's attitude to work according to age. The older group is slightly less ambitious, slightly more restless, and at the same time they adopt a slightly more responsible attitude to the necessity for work. 5% less of the older group say that they want to get to the top in their work: that is to say that 77% of those in their early twenties agree that this is the case, compared with 82% of those in their late teens. 5% more of the older group say that they frequently wish they could change their job: that is to say 28% of those in their early twenties frequently wish they could change their job, compared with 23% of those in their late teens. On the other hand, 68% of the older group disagree that they would rather go on Social Security than get a job they do not like doing, compared with 61% of the younger group.

LEISURE

The younger group are much less satisfied than the older group with the way in which they spend their leisure time. 12% more of the younger group say that they wish they had more things to do with their leisure.

As the young people mature, there seems to be a trend according to which they spend less time watching the television and more time reading books and newspapers. 8% less of those in their early twenties watch some television nearly every day, while 8% more of those in their early twenties say that they often read books. 74% of the older group read a newspaper nearly every day, compared with 67% of the younger group. Although, generally speaking, the older group watch less television, they take a significantly greater interest in the news broadcasts. 93% of the older group say that they listen to the radio or television news nearly every day, compared with 89% of the younger group.

Table 4.9   Leisure

	16–21 %	22–25 %
I wish I had more things to do with my leisure time	41	29
I often read books in my leisure time	71	79
I watch some television nearly every day	61	53
I often go drinking with my friends in my leisure time	49	57

Drinking becomes a significantly more prominent component of the leisure time activities among the older group. 8% more of those in their early twenties say that they often go drinking with their friends in their leisure time. The same proportion (95%) of both age groups agree that they often listen to music in their leisure time.

Sport plays a very similar role in the lives of both the age groups. Thus, 74% of the younger and 75% of the older groups take an active part in sport. 53% of the older and 52% of the younger often watch sport in their leisure time. Although sport seems to be of equal importance to the two age groups, it acts as a significantly stronger reason for joining the London Central YMCA among the older group. 94% of the older group say that they joined to use the sports facilities, compared with 88% of the younger group. At the same time, the social facilities are rated as a less important reason for joining by the older group. 36% of the older group joined to use the social facilities, compared with 42% of the younger group. 45% of the older group joined to meet people, compared with 58% of the younger group, and 35% of the older group joined to make friends, compared with 47% of the younger group.

Table 4.10   Leisure Facilities

	16-21 %	22-25 %
Facilities preferred by 22 - 25 age group		
Squash courts	47	53
Facilities preferred by 16 - 21 age group		
Badminton	54	49
Basket ball	23	12
Billiards, snooker, pool	40	27
Coffee bar	75	68
Dance classes	39	31
Disco	43	20
Filmshows	37	28
Gymnastics	24	15
Handball	8	3
Judo	13	6
Keep fit	38	33
Kuk sool won classes	8	1
Lounge area	49	36
Martial arts	14	7
Reading room	24	18
Slimmers classes	10	5
Soccer club	11	4
Table tennis	38	27
Tennis	28	16
Trampolining classes	17	8
Volley ball club	11	4
Weight training	35	27

In relationship to the leisure facilities and activities offered by London Central YMCA, the young people in their late teens show a slightly wider range of interests. On average, each member of the younger group checks an interest in eleven of the fifty two facilities or activities, and each member of the older group checks an interest in nine of them.

It is convenient to examine the relationship between age and leisure preferences in four stages. First, there are the minority activities which appeal to the same small proportion of both the sixteen to twenty-one and the twenty-two to twenty-five year age groups. In this category come the audio studio, Bible study, bridge, camping equipment, chapel, chess club, climbing equipment, craft workshop, cricket club, do-it-yourself classes, Duke of Edinburgh Award, exhibition facilities, mountaineering club, painting and drawing classes, newspaper production, rock climbing and slimnastics courses.

61

Second, there are those activities which appeal to a larger proportion, at least 10%, of the total membership, and the popularity of which is not significantly influenced by age. In this category come circuit training, darkroom, facials and massage, parachuting courses, photographic club, sauna, solarium, sports hall, sub-aqua club, swimming pool, swimming classes and yoga classes.

Third, there are the activities clearly more popular among the younger group. These are set out in table 4.10. This list includes not only many of the energetic pastimes, like badminton, gymnastics and weight training, but also the social facilities like the coffee bar and lounge, as well as the reading room and film shows.

Finally, there is just one activity which proves to be more popular among the older group than the younger - the squash courts.

COUNSELLING

The young people in their late teens tend to think of London as a more dangerous place in which to live than those in their early twenties. Significantly more of the younger group say that it is all too easy to get mixed up with prostitution and drugs in a place like London. In other ways, however, the young person's perceptions of London do not significantly differ during this age period. 55% of the younger and 56% of the older groups agree that London has a lot more to offer the young person than other cities. At the same time, 33% of the younger and 36% of the older groups think that the young person has to cope with more risks in London than in other cities. Only 12% of the younger and 8% of the older groups would not advise a young person to come to London to work or to study.

The young people in their late teens and those in their early twenties are both equally convinced of the need for counselling facilities in London. 62% of the younger group and 63% of the older group think that there should be more counselling facilities for young people in London.

Table 4.11   Counselling

	16-21 %	22-25 %
I think it is all too easy to get mixed up with drugs in a place like London	40	31
I think it is all too easy to get mixed up with prostitution in a place like London	31	20
I would never discuss my problems with a trained counsellor	23	18
I would never discuss my problems with a minister of religion	35	35

Significantly more of the older group, 78% compared with 73% of the younger group, say that from time to time they feel the need to talk their problems over with someone. Not only do the older group experience a greater need to discuss their problems, they also complain that they tend to receive less help when they do discuss them. 28% of the older group say they have not found it helpful to talk about their problems with their mother, compared with 23% of the younger group. 51% say that they have not derived help from their father, compared with 47% of the younger group. 64% of the older group say that they have not found it helpful to talk with a minister of religion, compared with 58% of the younger group. Similarly, 62% of the older group say that they have not derived help from a trained counsellor compared with 58% of the younger group.

The young person's perception of the usefulness of the trained counsellor differs with age. Significantly less of the older group claim that they would never discuss their problems with a trained counsellor. On the other hand, the young person's image of the usefulness of the minister of religion does not differ with age. Although the young people in their early twenties are more willing to draw upon the resources of the trained counsellor than those in their late teens, they do not become more willing to draw upon the resources of the minister of religion.

5 Students and Workers

This chapter is concerned with the younger respondents, aged twenty-one or less. It sets out to assess the differences between the 286 members in this age group who were workers and the 219 members who were students.

WELL-BEING

In many respects the students and young workers enjoy the same level of well-being. In relationship to ten of the twelve questions asked in this section, the responses of the two groups are not significantly different. At one end of the continuum of well-being, the same proportions of both groups say that they find life really worth living. This is the case for 87% of the workers and 84% of the students. At the other end of the continuum, the same proportions of both groups say they feel depressed and that they are not worth much as people. 20% of both groups claim that they tend to be lonely. 15% of the workers and 16% of the students feel that no-one knows them. 30% of both groups say that they often feel depressed. 49% of the workers and 50% of the students often long for someone to turn to for affection. 25% of the workers and 27% of the students often long for someone to turn to for advice.

In spite of all these similarities, the responses to the remaining two questions indicate two important differences between the young workers and the students. On the one hand, the students find that their lives have a greater sense of purpose. 79% of the students feel that their lives have a sense of purpose compared with 70% of the workers. On the other hand, the pressures of student life can be greater and more oppressive for young people than the pressures of a working life. Although at the time of completing the questionnaire only 3% more of the students, 15% compared with 12% of the workers, said that they were worried that they could not cope, the students were more aware that from time to time they experience pressures with which they were not equipped to cope. 25% of the students said that sometimes they had considered taking their own lives, compared with 18% of the workers.

WORRY

The students and the young workers are concerned by different sets of worries. The young workers tend to be more worried about financial matters and their own personal future. 5% more of the workers are worried about their debts, and 10% more are worried about growing old.

Similarly, 33% of the workers say that they are worried that they might get cancer, compared with 23% of the students.

Table 5.1   Worry

	Worker %	Student %
I am worried about the world situation	59	70
I often worry about my work	42	52
I am worried about my relationships with other people	22	28
I am worried about growing old	32	22
I am worried about my debts	24	19

The students tend to be more worried about their work and relationships, as well as about the general condition of the world in which they live. 11% more of the students are worried about the world situation. 10% more worry about their work, and 6% more are worried about their relationships with other people. A similar trend is shown in relationship to the question about the respondents' sex lives. 18% of the students say that they are worried about their sex lives, compared with 14% of the young workers.

There are only two issues on which the young workers and the students record the same levels of worry. 28% of both groups are worried about their health, and 11% of both groups say that they are worried that they might have a breakdown.

VALUES

Regarding economic values, students and workers attribute the same levels of importance to making money and to spending money. The workers give a higher value to saving money than the students. 77% of the workers say that saving money is important to them, compared with 70% of the students. In the long term, however, it is the students who attribute more importance to owning their own house. 79% of the students say that it is important for them to own their own house, compared with 72% of the workers.

Table 5.2   Values

	Worker %	Student %
My appearance is important to me	94	83
Religion is important to me	29	42
Moral values are important to me	79	74
Having a good time is more important than anything else	32	41
Politics is important to me	36	51

The students value both politics and religion more highly than the workers. 13% more of the students say that religion is important to them, and 15% more say that politics is important to them. On the other hand, the students attribute less importance to moral values. 5% less of the students say that moral values are important to them. The students also attribute less importance to their appearance and more importance to having a good time than the workers. 11% less of the students say that their appearance is important to them, and 9% more say that having a good time is more important than anything else.

Students and workers attribute the same value to their home, their family and their friends. Both groups find it equally important what other people think of them.

SELF IMAGE

In relationship to four of the seven issues concerned with their self image, the students and the young workers do not give significantly different responses. Nearly the same proportion of both groups admit to telling lies, breaking their promises and sometimes stealing things. Similarly, 70% of the students and 67% of the workers say that they are always willing to admit when they make a mistake.

Table 5.3   Self Image

	Worker %	Student %
Sometimes I have been jealous of others	80	67
Sometimes I feel resentful when I do not get my own way	60	72
Sometimes I have taken advantage of people	59	52

Where the two groups differ in their self image is in relationship to feelings of resentment, jealousy and taking advantage of others. 12% more of the students say that they sometimes feel resentful when they do not get their own way. On the other hand, it is the workers who tend to be more jealous and more frequently admit to taking advantage of other people.

BELIEFS

There is a lower proportion of agnostics and atheists among the student group. Thus, 10% of the students claim to be atheists, compared with 12% of the workers, while 26% of the students claim to be agnostic, compared with 30% of the workers. By way of comparison, 64% of the students say that they believe in God, compared with 58% of the workers. A closer examination of the religious affiliations of the two groups reveals that 66% of the workers and 59% of the students regard themselves as belonging to no particular religious group. 29% of the workers and 25% of the students claim affiliation to a Christian denomination. 5% of the workers and 16% of the students belong to another of the major world faiths. Thus, although more students than workers believe in God, 10% less students believe that Jesus Christ is the Son of God.

The students are much more likely than the young workers to have attended a place of worship and to have read the Bible within the last year. Thus, within the last year 65% of the students have attended a place of worship compared with 51% of the workers, while 43% of the students have read the Bible within the last year, compared with 32% of the workers. However, there is no significant difference in the proportions of the two groups who dismiss both the Bible and the church as irrelevant. 23% of both groups say that the Bible seems irrelevant for life today, and 23% of the workers and 20% of the students say that the church seems irrelevant for life today. Similarly, there is no significant difference between the proportions of the two groups who claim to take an active part in a church. 6% of the young workers and 7% of the students take an active part in church.

Table 5.4   Beliefs

	Worker %	Student %
I believe that Jesus Christ is the Son of God	52	42
I believe that luck plays an important part in my life	50	44
I believe in my horoscope	25	17
I think religious education should be taught in schools	63	52

There are no significant differences in the proportions of the workers and the students who pray or believe either in life after death or in reincarnation. 32% of the students and 31% of the workers have prayed within the past week. 47% of the students and 48% of the workers believe in life after death. 26% of the students and 28% of the workers believe in reincarnation.

Although the workers hold less belief than the students in conventional aspects of religion, they tend to hold more belief in aspects of superstition. Thus, 8% more of the workers say that they believe in their horoscope. Similarly, 6% more of the workers say that they believe that luck plays an important part in their lives. 55% of the workers believe that there is intelligent life on other planets, compared with 50% of the students.

Interestingly, although more of the students believe in God, go to places of worship and read the Bible, it is the workers rather than the students who tend to support the provision of religious education in schools. 11% more of the workers say that they think religious education should be taught in schools.

MORALS

It is the student group which emerges as consistently more traditional in its moral outlook regarding sexual ethics. 10% of the student group say that it is wrong for an unmarried couple to live together, compared with 5% of the workers. 14% of the students think it is wrong to have sexual intercourse outside marriage, compared with 10% of the workers. 5% of the students think contraception is wrong, compared with 2% of the workers. Similarly, the students are much more strongly against homosexuality than the workers.

Regarding their attitudes towards alcohol and drugs, the students emerge as more conservative in relationship to their attitude towards alcohol and more liberal in their attitude towards heroin. About the same proportion of both groups think that it is wrong to use marijuana.

Table 5.5   Morals

	Worker %	Student %
I think the practice of homosexuality is wrong	22	40
I think it is wrong to become drunk	29	43
I think it is wrong to use heroin	79	71
I think abortion is wrong	11	19

There is no significant difference in the proportion of students (25%) and workers (26%) who think that euthanasia is wrong. However, significantly more students think that abortion is wrong, 19% compared with 11% of the workers, while more workers think that war is wrong, 64% compared with 59% of the students.

LAW

The young workers and the students hold very similar attitudes towards the law. In relationship to the motoring law, the same proportions of both groups consider that parking restrictions should be strictly obeyed, that speed limits should be strictly obeyed, and that it is wrong to drink and drive. Also both groups hold quite similar attitudes towards such issues as fraud. There is no significant difference in the proportions of the two groups who say that it is alright to travel without a ticket, to smuggle an extra bottle of spirits through the customs, or to falsify tax returns.

POLITICS

The student group takes a more active part in politics than the young workers. Compared with the workers nearly three times the proportion of students claim to take an active part in politics. The students are also less sceptical about politics. 10% less of the students say that it does not matter which political party is in power.

Larger proportions of the student group support both the Labour party and the Liberal party. Conversely, the Conservative party receives less support from the student group. This pattern of party political affiliation is also strongly reflected in the different attitudes held by the two groups towards specific political issues. The students are more left wing. 29% of the students think that the nationalisation of industry is a good thing, compared with 14% of the young workers. 18% of the students think that private medicine should be abolished, compared with 11% of the workers. 13% of the students think that private schools should be abolished, compared with 8% of the workers. Similarly, the students are less critical of the trade unions. 64% of the students think that the trade unions have too much power, compared with 74% of the workers.

The students are more open to accepting Britain as part of the European Economic Community. 42% of the students think that the Common Market is a good thing, compared with 32% of the workers. The workers' concern to protect their home economy is very much greater than the students' concern for this issue. 75% of the workers think that immigration into Britain should be restricted, compared with 41% of the students. When it comes to positively supporting home industry, the workers are not significantly more actively involved than the students. 16% of the workers and 14% of the students say they would rather buy a British car than one made in another country. The students are more concerned about the implications of the influence of international corporations. 44% of the students think that too much power is in the hands of multinational corporations, compared with 35% of the workers.

Table 5.6   Politics

	Worker %	Student %
I take an active part in politics	4	11
It makes no difference which political party is in power	32	22
I have confidence in the policies of the Labour party	10	20
I have confidence in the policies of the Conservative party	29	23
I have confidence in the policies of the Liberal party	4	10

The six questions which ask the respondents to rate whether they consider nurses, doctors, policemen, car workers, miners and clergy as underpaid for the job they do reveal a very significant difference between the students and the young workers. In relationship to each of these six questions, a considerably higher proportion of the students opt for the not certain response. For example 40% of the students say that they are not certain whether nurses are underpaid for the job they do, compared with 15% of the workers. The students are both less aware of the salaries actually being paid for these jobs, and also less willing to make judgements about the economic worth of different groups.

SOCIETY

In relationship to ten of the fifteen issues of social concern reviewed by this survey, there are no significant differences in the responses of the students and the young workers. The two groups register the same levels of concern about the efficiency of the health service, the divorce rate, violence on television, the crime rate, pollution to the environment, the rate of inflation, homelessness, unemployment and nuclear war. In summary, 23% of the workers and 25% of the students say that they do not see much future for Britain.

The five areas of social concern regarding which the two groups differ reveal some interesting characteristics which distinguish the students from the young workers. The two groups have different views about education and about money. The student group can be considered as those who benefited well from the current system of schooling. 18% less of the students consider that the educational standard of schools is declining. The workers are those who are now more likely to be actively involved in the world of earning money and material possessions. 9% more of the workers believe that the credit card encourages careless spending. It is the students and not the workers who are the more concerned about the poverty of the third world.

Table 5.7   Society

	Worker %	Student %
I believe that the educational standard of schools is declining	70	52
I believe that the credit card encourages careless spending	49	40
I believe that pornography is too readily available	49	43
I believe that it is becoming too easy to obtain an abortion	23	31
I am concerned about the poverty of the third world	59	71

Finally, the students and workers differ in their evaluation of the moral climate of Britain. The students are more concerned about the issue of abortion: the workers are more concerned about pornography.

WORK

There is a predictable difference in the level of income enjoyed by the students and the workers. The average weekly income for the students is £38.50, while for the workers it is £51.90. A much higher proportion of the students (41%) exist on less than £40 per week, compared with 6% of the workers.

The students are more likely to say that they are happy in their work than the workers. Only 5% of the students say that they are not happy in what they are doing compared with 11% of the young workers. Similarly, 17% less of the students claim that they frequently wish they could change their job in order to do something other than what they are doing. On the other hand, the students are considerably more likely than the workers to say that they often worry about their work. The students also reveal more ambition associated with their work than the workers. 8% more of the students say that they want to get to the top in their work.

Table 5.8   Work

	Worker %	Student %
I want to get to the top in my job	78	86
I often worry about my work	42	52
Frequently I wish I could change my job	31	14
I would rather go on social security than get a job I do not like doing	16	21

The fact that the students have become more accustomed to greater satisfaction in their work makes them more reluctant to accept situations in which they are not likely to receive a sufficient level of job satisfaction. 5% more of the students say that they would rather go on Social Security than get a job they do not like doing.

LEISURE

Both the students and the young workers experience an equally high level of dissatisfaction with the current use of their leisure time. 42% of the workers and 40% of the students say that they wish they had more things to do with their leisure time.

In many ways, the students and workers seem to adopt very similar attitudes to leisure time activities. The same proportions of both groups read books, listen to music, watch television, listen to the news and either play or watch sport. There are just two activities in which the students take less interest than the workers. 8% less of the students read a news-paper every day: 17% less often go drinking with their friends. It is likely that the different levels of participation in both of these activities is related to the expense of buying papers and going drinking.

Table 5.9   Leisure

	Worker %	Student %
I wish I had more things to do with my leisure time	42	40
I watch some television nearly every day	60	62
I often go drinking with my friends in my leisure time	57	40
I read a newspaper nearly everyday	70	62

The students and the young workers give very similar reasons for joining London Central YMCA. Both groups give a very high priority to the use of the sports facilities. Similarly, about the same proportion of both groups, that is to say 45% of the workers and 47% of the students, report that they join to make friends.

The students and the young workers take an interest in an equal range of the facilities and activities offered by London Central YMCA. The members of both groups check on average an interest in eleven of the fifty-two activities or facilities listed in the questionnaire.

The students take a greater interest than the workers in nine areas. 6% of the students are interested in bridge, compared with 1% of the workers. 16% of the students are interested in chess, compared with 8% of the workers. 34% of the students show an interest in the reading room, compared with 15% of the workers. The students are also more interested in table tennis and billiards, basketball and the martial arts, the darkroom and film shows.

The workers also take a greater interest than the students in nine other areas. 51% of the young workers wish to use the lounge area, compared with 44% of the students. 56% of the workers are interested in the sauna, compared with 40% of the students. 90% of the workers are interested in the swimming pool, compared with 82% of the students. The young workers are also more interested in badminton, the solarium, facials and massage, dance classes, trampolining classes and keep fit.

The two groups take an equal interest in the audio studio, Bible study, camping equipment, chapel, circuit training, climbing equipment, coffee bar, craft workshop, cricket club, disco, do-it-yourself classes, Duke of Edinburgh award scheme, exhibition facilities, gymnastics, handball, judo, kuk sool won classes, mountaineering club, painting and drawing classes, parachuting courses, newspaper production, photographic club, rock climbing, slimnastics courses, slimming classes, soccer club, sports hall, squash courts, sub-aqua club, swimming classes, tennis, volleyball club, weight training and yoga classes.

COUNSELLING

The student group feels more threatened by London than the young workers. 8% of the students say that they hate London, compared with 3% of the workers. 5% more of the students say that they would not advise a young person to come to London to work or to study. The student group tends to think that the young person has to cope with more risks in London than in other cities. 10% more of the students think that it is all too easy to get mixed up with prostitution in a place like London. On the other hand, exactly the same proportion of students and workers (40%) think that it is all too easy to get mixed up with drugs in London. 5% more of the young students say that there should be more counselling facilities for young people in London.

Table 5.10   Counselling

	Worker %	Student %
I would not advise a young person to come to London to work or study	9	14
I think there should be more counselling facilities for young people in London	60	65
I think it is all too easy to get mixed up with prostitution in a place like London	27	37
I have found it helpful to talk about my problems with a minister of religion	11	17
I have found it helpful to talk about my problems with a trained counsellor	7	14

The same proportions of the students and the young workers (72%) say that from time to time they need to talk their problems over with someone. The same proportions of both groups have found it helpful to talk about their problems with their close friends, their mother and their father. Where there is a significant difference in the two groups is in relationship to their experience of the helping professions. 14% of the students have found it helpful to talk about their problems with a trained counsellor, compared with 7% of the workers. 17% of the students have found it helpful to talk with a minister of religion, compared with 11% of the workers. Nevertheless, similar proportions of the two groups remain unwilling to seek help from members of these caring professions. 23% of the workers and 24% of the students say that they would never discuss their problems with a trained counsellor. 37% of the workers and 34% of the students say they would never discuss their problems with a minister of religion.

6 Employment and Unemployment

In order to assess the relationship between the experience of unemployment and the attitudes of the sixteen to twenty-five year olds who responded to the questionnaire, the total sample was divided into three categories – those who had experienced no unemployment in the last two years, those who had experienced some unemployment during the last two years but for a total period not exceeding six months, and those who had experienced more than six months unemployment during the past two years. 68.5% of the sample had experienced no unemployment. 21.5% had experienced up to six months unemployment and the remaining 10% had experienced between seven and twenty-four months unemployment. In the following discussion I shall adopt the practice of referring to these groups as those which have experienced no unemployment, some unemployment and much unemployment, and to the people who constitute these groups as the employed, the short-term unemployed and the long-term unemployed.

WELL-BEING

There is a very clear relationship between the young people's experience of unemployment and their psychological well-being. Unemployment seems to be related to lower self-confidence and greater restlessness, despondency and despair. The unemployed tend to be more dissatisfied with life in general and to long more for changes.

Significantly more of those who have been unemployed for a long time say that they are lonely and that that no-one knows them. 25% of those who have experienced much unemployment say that they tend to be lonely compared with 20% of those who have experienced no unemployment. 19% of the long-term unemployed say that they feel no-one knows them, compared with 14% of the employed. Similarly, 12% of the long-term unemployed say that they feel that they are not worth much as people, compared with 6% of the employed. The proportion who say that they do not find life worth living increases from 3% to 8%, and the proportion who say that their lives have no sense of purpose increases from 7% to 9%.

Another index of the insecurity related to unemployment is that 65% of the long-term unemployed say that they like to have a lot of people around them, compared with 58% of the employed. 30% of the long-term unemployed long for someone to turn to for advice, compared with 23% of the employed. Similarly, 9% more of the long-term unemployed say that they long for someone to turn to for affection.

Table 6.1   Well-being

	months	0 %	1- 6 %	7-24 %
I often long for someone to turn to for advice		23	25	30
I often long for someone to turn to for affection		46	52	55
I often feel depressed		24	34	34
I am worried that I cannot cope		11	15	17
I have sometimes considered taking my own life		17	24	26

These feelings in turn lead to increased anxiety and depression. 10% more of the long term unemployed say that they often feel depressed. 17% of the long term unemployed say that they are worried that they cannot cope, compared with 11% of the employed. An extra 9% of the long-term unemployed said that they have sometimes considered taking their own life.

WORRY

The unemployed generally tend to worry about things significantly more than the employed. Unemployment is related to extra worry about the whole area of work: 10% more of the long-term unemployed are worried about their work. Reduced income causes the unemployed to worry more about their debts:9% more of the long-term unemployed are worried about their debts.

This increased level of worry is carried over into other areas of life as well, like health and relationships. 29% of the long-term unemployed are worried about their health, compared with 24% of the employed. 8% more of the long-term unemployed are worried about growing old. Similarly 8% more of the long-term unemployed are worried that they might have a breakdown. 24% of the unemployed say that they are worried about their relationships, compared with 21% of the employed, and 5% more of the long-term unemployed are worried about their sex lives.

Table 6.2   Worry

	months	0 %	1- 6 %	7-24 %
I am worried about my debts		20	23	29
I often worry about my work		44	44	54
I am worried about growing old		26	29	34
I am worried about my sex life		14	18	19
I am worried I might have a breakdown		8	12	16

Only in relationship to two of the nine questions about worry do the unemployed not register a significantly higher level of anxiety than the employed. The unemployed are not more worried about the world situation, nor are they more worried that they might get cancer.

VALUES

There is a clear, curvilinear relationship between the experience of unemployment and economic values. A short period of unemployment is related to a lessening of the importance that money plays in the young person's life. The short-term unemployed ascribe significantly less importance to making money, saving money and spending money than the employed. The long-term unemployed, however, who have presumably incurred greater financial hardship, reassert the importance of money in their lives. In particular it becomes important to them to have more money to spend. This pattern is reproduced in the importance the respondents attach to owning their own house. 76% of the employed and 73% of the long-term unemployed say that it is important for them to own their own house, compared with 65% of the short-term unemployed.

The young person's sense of personal value is significantly related to the experience of unemployment. 8% less of the long-term unemployed say that what people think of them is important to them. Similarly, 86% of the unemployed say their appearance is important to them compared with 91% of the employed. By way of compensation, the unemployed tend to seek pleasures more readily: more of the unemployed agree that having a good time is more important than anything else.

Table 6.3   Values

	months	0 %	1-6 %	7-24 %
Making money is important to me		67	62	70
Saving money is important to me		74	65	72
Spending money is important to me		55	53	61
What people think of me is important to me		73	70	65
Having a good time is more important than anything else		33	30	40

On the other hand, the experience of unemployment bears no relationship to the importance the young person attaches to politics, religion or moral values. Nor is the value ascribed to home, family or friends influenced at all by unemployment.

SELF IMAGE

The long-term unemployed are significantly more defensive than the employed. Possibly in order to compensate for the erosion of their sense of personal worth identified in the previous section, they try harder to present a socially desirable image of themselves. 8% more of the long-term unemployed claim that they have never told a lie. Significantly less of the long-term unemployed admit to having taken advantage of other people or to feelings of jealousy. Similarly, 73% of the long-term unemployed say that they are always willing to admit when they make a mistake compared with 67% of the employed.

Table 6.4   Self Image

	months	0 %	1- 6 %	7-24 %
Sometimes I have been jealous of others		79	82	70
I have never told a lie		3	3	11
Sometimes I have taken advantage of people		62	61	55
I am always willing to admit when I make a mistake		67	72	73

On the other hand, the percentage responses to the other three of the seven issues in this section do not seem to be related to the experience of unemployment. The same proportion of the employed and the unemployed say that they sometimes feel resentful when they do not get their own way, that they have never broken their promise and that they have never stolen anything in their lives.

BELIEFS

There is no clearly discernible pattern between unemployment and religious belief. 57% of the employed, 56% of the short-term unemployed and 59% of the long-term unemployed claimed to believe in God. 44% of the employed, 47% of the short-term unemployed and 43% of the long-term unemployed believe that Jesus Christ is the Son of God. Similarly, there is no significant difference between the employed and the long-term unemployed in terms of their church attendance, their active involvement in the church or their attitude towards the church. 26% of the employed and 23% of the long-term unemployed say that the church seems irrelevant for life today. Unemployment appears to direct towards religion neither greater dependency nor greater rejection.

The experience of unemployment is also unrelated to the faith the young people place in their horoscope or the extent to which they feel their lives are directed by luck. 17% of the employed and 20% of the unemployed believe in their horoscope. 50% of the employed and 50% of the unemployed say that they believe that luck plays an important life in their lives.

MORALS

Just as there is no clear relationship between unemployment and religious belief, so there is no clear relationship between unemployment and morals. The experience of unemployment leads neither to greater moral liberalisation nor to greater moral conservatism. Those who have experienced much unemployment tend to respond to questions about sexual ethics, the sanctity of life and drugs in very much the same way as those who have been fully employed. The one major exception to this generalisation concerns the question about alcohol. The unemployed tend to adopt a significantly stricter attitude towards drunkenness. 39% of the long-term unemployed argue that it is wrong to become drunk, compared with 31% of the short-term unemployed and 29% of the employed.

LAW

The area in which unemployment is related to the young person's attitude to law is that directely concerned with money. The shortage of money brought about by unemployment seems to result in the young re-evaluating where they stand on issues relating to money and the law. 25% of the long-term unemployed agree that it is not wrong to travel without a ticket, compared with 21% of the short-term unemployed and 19% of the employed. Only 47% of the long-term unemployed argue that tax returns should be filled in with complete honesty, compared with 55% of the short-term unemployed and 54% of the employed.

The long-term unemployed young person's greater willingness to evade the law on financial issues does not seem to be generalised into a more pervading contempt for or hostility towards the law. Almost exactly the same proportion of the long-term unemployed and the employed say that it is wrong to bring an extra bottle of spirits through the customs or to sell cigarettes to children under the legal age. Regarding the motoring laws, the long-term unemployed and the employed agree on the issues of parking restrictions and drinking and driving. On the issue of speed limits, the unemployed adopt a more rigorous attitude than the employed. 70% of the long-term unemployed say that speed limits should be strictly obeyed, compared with 64% of the short-term unemployed and 60% of the employed.

POLITICS

Generally speaking, the political views of the short-term unemployed do not differ greatly from those of the employed. However, the experience of long-term unemployment does have a clear relationship with the young person's attitude towards politics. Politics seems more important to the long-term unemployed young people as a way of changing their situation. 12% of the long-term unemployed say that they take an active part in politics, compared with 7% of the employed and 5% of the short-term unemployed. Instead of leading to increased apathy towards politics, the experience of long-term unemployment seems to encourage the young person to believe that a political solution could have a positive effect on the situation. Significantly less of the long-term unemployed argue that it makes no difference which political party is in power. Thus, only 23% of the long-term unemployed say that it makes no difference which political party is. in power, compared with 31% of the short-term unemployed and 29% of the employed.

The differences in party political allegiance displayed by the employed and the unemployed is also very significant. The same proportions of the employed and the unemployed support the Labour party. Less of the long-term unemployed support the Conservative party. The party which attracts significantly more support from the long-term unemployed is the Liberal party.

The tendency for the long-term unemployed not to support the policies of the Conservative party is also illustrated by the percentage responses to specific questions. More of the long-term unemployed think that private schools should be abolished. Less of the long-term unemployed believe that the trade unions have too much power. On the other hand, unemployment is not significantly related to enthusiasm for the nationalisation of industry or the abolition of private medicine. 21% of the long-term unemployed and 19% of the employed think that the nationalisation of industry is a good thing. 17% of the long-term unemployed and 15% of the employed think that private medicine should be abolished.

Table 6.5   Politics

months	0 %	1- 6 %	7-24 %
I have confidence in the policies of the Labour party	17	17	16
I have confidence in the policies of the Conservative party	27	30	22
I have confidence in the policies of the Liberal party	7	8	13
I think the trade unions have too much power	72	68	65
I think private schools should be abolished	10	11	19

The long-term unemployed do not appear to have adopted protectionist policies towards jobs in Britain, either by supporting home industry or by attempting to exclude foreign workers. Only 12% of the long-term unemployed say that they would rather buy a British car than one made in another country, compared with 18% of the employed. 49% of the long-term unemployed think that the Common Market is a good thing, compared with 45% of the employed. 59% of the long-term unemployed argue that immigration into Britain should be restricted, compared with 64% of the employed.

Finally, the experience of unemployment bears no relationship with the way in which the young evaluate the pay claims of nurses, policemen, car workers, miners or clergy. There is, however, a significant relationship between unemployment and the young person's evaluation of doctors. Only 48% of the long-term unemployed think that doctors are underpaid for the job they do, compared with 58% of the employed.

SOCIETY

In most of the areas of social concern reviewed by the survey there are no significant differences in the percentage responses of the employed and the unemployed groups. All three groups are equally concerned about the crime rate, the educational standards of schools, the efficiency of the health service, the ease with which it is currently possible to obtain abortion or divorce, the availability of pornography, the risks of pollution and nuclear war, and the problems of homelessness. While the two groups register the same levels of concern for all these issues relevant to contemporary life in Britain, the long-term unemployed rate the overall implications of these concerns more seriously. In comparison both with the employed and the short-term unemployed, 8% more of the long-term unemployed say that they do not see much future for Britain.

Interestingly, it is those who have experienced short-term unemployment who are most concerned about the problems of unemployment. Those who have experienced long-term unemployment seem to have become hardened to the issue and no longer rate it so highly as a matter of concern. It is concern with issues related to the financial implications of unemployment, rather than concern with the problems of unemployment itself, which distinguish the long-term unemployed group most clearly from the employed group. The long-term unemployed are both much less concerned about the rate of inflation, and at the same time much more concerned that the credit card encourages careless spending.

Table 6.6   Society

	months	0 %	1- 6 %	7-24 %
I do not see much future for Britain		23	22	31
I am concerned about the problems of unemployment		73	80	69
I believe that the credit card encourages careless spending		45	43	51
I am concerned about the rate of inflation		82	83	74
I believe that there is too much violence on television		29	40	40

The final issue of social concern on which the employed and the unemployed differ concerns the level of violence portrayed on television. The unemployed groups are significantly more concerned about this problem and more of them tend to believe that there is too much violence on television. Perhaps the unemployed have allowed themselves to become more exposed to what is shown on television, and therefore react more strongly against it.

WORK

There are some significant differences in the attitude towards work of those who have not experienced unemployment and those who have experienced periods of unemployment. Those who have experienced long-term unemployment tend to be generally less well-suited to their work and to derive less satisfaction from working. 15% less of the long-term unemployed say that they like the people that they work with. 6% more of the long-term unemployed frequently wish that they could change their job. Similarly only 69% of the long-term unemployed report that they are happy in their work, compared with 73% of those who have experienced no unemployment.

Those who have experienced either short-term or long-term unemployment tend to attach less importance to work itself: 4% less say that they think it is important to work hard. At the same time 12% more say that they would rather go on social security than get a job they do not like doing.

Table 6.7   Work

	months	0 %	1- 6 %	7-24 %
I like the people I work with		86	81	71
Frequently I wish I could change my job		26	27	32
I think it is important to work hard		88	84	84
I would rather go on social security than get a job I do not like doing		15	24	27

LEISURE

Not only do the long-term unemployed hold less positive attitudes towards their work, they also hold less positive attitudes towards their leisure. The long-term unemployed seem to be young people who have less interest in life. 7% more of the unemployed say that they wish they had more things to do in their leisure time. This is not simply a reflection on the fact that the unemployed have more leisure time, but also that they seem to have interest in less leisure time activities. 12% less of the long-term unemployed read a newspaper nearly every day. 6% less listen to the radio or television news nearly every day. 10% less take an active part in sport, and 14% less often watch sport in their leisure time. On the other hand, the employed and the unemployed seem to take an equal interest in reading books, watching television, listening to music and going drinking with their friends. Similarly, there are no significant differences in the facilities and activities offered by London Central YMCA which appeal to the employed and unemployed groups.

Table 6.8   Leisure

	months	0 %	1- 6 %	7-24 %
I wish I had more things to do with my leisure time		32	32	39
I read a newspaper nearly every day		74	68	62
I take an active part in sport		77	70	67
I often watch sport in my leisure time		58	39	44

COUNSELLING

The experience of long-term unemployment seems to help to increase the young person's perception of the problems of living in London. London is a good city for the young people who succeed: it is an unsatisfactory environment for those who do not succeed. The long-term unemployed are significantly less certain than the employed that London has more to offer the young person than other cities. At the same time, they are more aware of the need for counselling facilities for young people in London.

The long-term unemployed themselves have apparently had more contact with professional counselling. They have derived significantly more help than the other young people from talking about their problems both with ministers of religion and trained counsellors. Similarly, only 18% of the long-term unemployed say that they would never discuss their problems with a trained counsellor, compared with 23% of those who have experienced no unemployment; and 32% of the unemployed say they would never discuss their problems with a minister of religion, compared with 37% of the employed.

Table 6.9   Counselling

	months	0 %	1- 6 %	7-24 %
I think London has a lot more to offer the young person than other cities		57	56	48
I think there should be more counselling facilities for young people in London		61	63	69
I have found it helpful to talk about my problems with a minister of religion		11	8	19
I have found it helpful to talk about my problems with a trained counsellor		9	14	20

The fact that twice as many of the long-term unemployed have derived help from both counsellors and clergy is especially revealing in the light of another statistical comparison. The same proportions of the employed and unemployed have found it helpful to discuss their problems with their mother, father and close friends. It is only in relationship to the caring professions that the experience of the unemployed differs from that of the employed. This seems to highlight the importance of the availability of professional counselling facilities for the young unemployed in Central London.

7 British and Foreign

In order to illustrate the differences in the attitudes and values between
the young people born in Britain and those born overseas, the sample was
divided into three groups, the 680 British born members, the 141 foreign
born members who had lived in Britain for more than five years, and the
239 foreign born members who had lived in Britain for less than five years.
In the following discussion these three groups will be referred to as the
British, the established foreign, and the unestablished foreign groups. This
analysis helps to highlight the special situation of the young people who are
not yet established in London or in the British way of life.

WELL-BEING

There is a very clear relationship between length of residence in Britain
and the young person's sense of psychological well-being. As is to be
expected, it is those who are actually born in Britain who experience
the greatest degree of psychological well-being living in London. London
places a greater strain on those living in it as a host culture than on those
who were born in this country. The foreign born young people who have
lived in Britain for more than five years are also considerably better
adapted to life in London than the unestablished foreign members. 21%
more of the British members say that they like living in England: 8% more
say that they find life really worth living.

The difference between the two groups seems to be a result of the
environment rather than the reflection of their basic character. The
British and the foreign groups have a very similar sense of purpose in
their lives: 72% of the British and 75% of the foreign members say that
their lives have a sense of purpose. Both groups take an equal responsibility for their own lives: 49% of both groups say that luck plays an
important part in their lives. Both groups are equally well suited to city
living: similar proportions of both groups say that they find crowds
oppressive or they like to have a lot of people around them.

The real difference between the two groups is that the foreigners
naturally feel less at home and more isolated. This in turn is related to
their ability to relate to people and their own self evaluation. 11% more
of the foreigners say that they tend to be lonely. Similarly, 18% of the
foreigners say that they feel no-one knows them compared with 14% of the
British. 17% more of the foreigners say that they often long for someone
to turn to for advice. Similarly, 55% of the unestablished foreigners say
that they often long for someone to turn to for affection, compared with

50% of the established foreigners and 47% of the British.

Table 7. 1   Well- being

	life %	over 5 yrs%	under 5 yrs%
I find life really worth living	87	81	79
I like living in England	79	73	58
I tend to be a lonely person	19	22	30
I often long for someone to turn to for advice	19	33	36
I have sometimes considered taking my own life	17	15	24

More of the unestablished foreigners doubt their own self worth.   10% of the unestablished foreigners say that they feel they are not worth much as a person, compared with 6% of the established foreigners and 5% of the British.   18% of the unestablished foreigners are worried that they cannot cope, compared with 11% of the British and 11% of the established foreigners 34% of the unestablished foreigners say that they often feel depressed, compared with 30% of the established foreigners and 26% of the British.

The conclusion that it is the unestablished foreigners who are most at risk in Central London is confirmed by the significantly greater proportion of them who say that they have sometimes considered taking their own lives.

WORRY

The level of worry about a whole variety of things is significantly higher among the unestablished foreigners than among the British or the established foreigners.   This higher level of worry seems to be associated with the stresses of becoming established in a foreign culture.   The unestablished f oreign group are more worried about their work, their relationships and their health.   25% of the unestablished foreigners are worried about their debts, compared with 21% of the British, and 18% are worried about their sex lives, compared with 14% of the British.   The all pervasive nature of this worry is indicated by the fact that 70% of the foreigners say that they are worried about the world situation, compared with 62% of the British.

Table 7. 2   Worry

	life %	over 5 yrs%	under 5 yrs%
I often worry about my work	44	43	50
I am worried about my relationships with other people	20	18	30
I am worried that I might have a breakdown	8	11	15
I am worried about my health	23	22	34
I am worried that I might get cancer	37	27	25

Although significantly more of the unestablished foreigners are worried about their health, it is the British who tend to be more frightened of cancer. It is interesting to note that the level of worry exhibited by the established foreigners matches that of the British in relationship to the issue of their health in general, but matches the unestablished foreigners in relationship to the specific issue of cancer. Anxiety about cancer seems to be something to which the British are particularly susceptible.

VALUES

There is an interesting difference in the economic values of the British and foreign groups. Both groups attribute a similar level of importance to making money and to saving money. The British group, however, attributes much more importance to spending money, while the foreign group looks more to the future. 79% of the foreigners say that it is important for them to own their own house, compared with 71% of the British.

The three groups place the same high value on their home, family and friends. The British and foreign young people also attribute the same level of importance to their work and to moral values. On the other hand, the foreign young people rate both religion and politics more highly than British young people. Thus, in comparison with the British born group, 26% more of the unestablished foreign group say that religion is important to them, while 10% more of the unestablished foreign group say that politics is important to them.

Table 7. 3   Values

	life %	over 5 yrs%	under 5 yrs%
My appearance is important to me	93	91	79
Spending money is important to me	58	52	46
Having a good time is more important than anything else	29	34	43
Religion is important to me	25	34	51
Politics is important to me	44	49	54

Where there is another significant difference in the value structure of the British and the foreign young people is in relationship to their self evaluation. It seems that the isolation which foreigners experience in the host country reduces their contact with other people and consequently changes the extent to which they are able to draw on others for confirmation of their own worth. 66% of the unestablished foreigners say that what people think of them is important, compared with 72% of the established foreigners and 74% of the British. Similarly, significantly less of the unestablished foreigners are concerned about their appearance. The foreign members tend to compensate for this by seeking other pleasures. 14% more of the unestablished foreigners say that having a good time is more important than anything else.

SELF IMAGE

The greater insecurity of the foreign members inevitably leads them to try to project a more socially desirable image of themselves. For example, in comparison with the British born young people, 10% more of the unestablished foreign group claim that they have never told a lie, while 11% more of the unestablished foreign group claim that they have never broken their promise. Similarly, in comparison with the British born group, 18% less of the unestablished foreigners admit to feelings of jealousy, while 19% less of the unestablished foreigners admit to having taken advantage of others. On the other hand, there is no difference in the proportions of the groups who admit to stealing or to feelings of resentment.

Table 7.4   Self Image

	life %	over 5 yrs%	under 5 yrs%
Sometimes I have been jealous of others	83	68	65
I have never told a lie	2	4	10
I have never broken a promise	19	24	30
Sometimes I have taken advantage of people	66	52	47

BELIEFS

The unestablished foreign group has a much higher level of belief in God than the British group, and the established foreign group holds a position almost exactly between the other two. 73% of the unestablished foreign young people say that they believe in God, compared with 61% of the established foreign group and 51% of the British born group. Only 9% of the unestablished foreigners claim to be atheists, compared with 13% of the established foreigners and 16% of the British. Similarly only 18% of the unestablished foreigners claim to be agnostics, compared with 26% of the established foreigners and 33% of the British. The longer the young people have lived in England, the less likely they are to believe in God.

60% of the foreigners say that they do not belong to any religious group, compared with 69% of the British members. Although the same proportion of British and foreign members believe that Jesus Christ is the Son of God, a lower proportion of the foreign members actually claim to hold allegiance to a Christian church. 25% of the foreigners belong to a Christian church, compared with 29% of the British. A greater proportion of the foreign Christians are Roman Catholic, 15% compared with 8% of the British. A greater proportion of the British Christians are Church of England, 17% compared with 5% of the foreigners.

15% of the foreign members belong to one of the other world faiths. Of these, 9% are Moslem and 2% are Buddhists. The only world faith apart from Christianity significantly represented amongst those born in Britain is Judaism, which accounts for 4% of the British members.

The foreign group also exhibits more religious behaviour in terms of

a higher level of prayer and more attendance at places of worship.
Thus 61% of the foreigners say that they have been to a place of worship
within the last year, compared with 51% of the British young people.
Similarly, 71% of the foreigners say that they have prayed within the last
year, compared with 57% of the British young people. These are activities
which are not peculiar to the practice of the Christian faith. The more
distinctively Christian activity of Bible reading is not practised more by the
foreign group than by the British group.

The greater belief in God claimed by the foreign members is strangely
not reflected in their responses to the other questions concerning religious
belief. The same proportions of the British and foreign members believe
in reincarnation as well as in life after death. 58% of both the foreign
and the British groups think that religious education should be taught in
schools.

Regarding their secular beliefs, more of the British tend to believe
that there is intelligent life on other planets, 56% compared with 49% of
the established foreigners and 43% of the unestablished foreigners. The
same proportions of the British and foreign members believe both in their
horoscope and that luck plays an important part in their lives.

MORALS

There is a considerable difference in the sexual ethics of the British and
foreign members. The unestablished foreigners adopt a more conservative
stand on the issues of contraception, extra-marital intercourse, homosexuality and abortion. 7% more of the unestablished foreigners think that
abortion is wrong, 12% more think that extra-marital intercourse is wrong
and 28% more think that homosexuality is wrong. The established foreigners
report attitudes much closer to the British norms.

Table 7. 5   Morals

	life %	over 5 yrs%	under 5 yrs%
I think contraception is wrong	1	1	8
I think it is wrong for an unmarried couple to live together	4	4	13
I think it is wrong to have sexual intercourse outside marriage	7	13	19
I think the practice of homosexuality is wrong	16	31	44
I think abortion is wrong	10	16	25

Regarding the use of alcohol and drugs, the British and foreign members
adopt a very similar attitude towards heroin. In relationship to marijuana
and alcohol the foreign members adopt a stricter attitude than the British
members. 55% of the unestablished foreigners think it is wrong to use
marijuana, compared with 44% of the established foreigners and 31% of the
British. 53% of the unestablished foreigners think it is wrong to become
drunk, compared with 22% of the British and 49% of the established
foreigners.

LAW

The unestablished foreigners are less certain about the risks which they can take in relationship to the law in Britain. The foreigners who have lived in Britain for more than five years have tended to adopt attitudes towards the law which are much closer to those of the British. The unestablished foreigners adopt a more cautious attitude to the taxation authority and the customs officers. On the other hand, the same proportions of the British and foreign young people are willing to condone travelling without a ticket.

Table 7.6   Law

	life %	over 5 yrs%	under 5 yrs%
There is nothing wrong in bringing an extra bottle of spirits through the customs if you are not caught	46	45	34
I think tax returns should be filled in with complete honesty	51	52	59
There is nothing wrong with drinking and driving if you can get away with it	4	6	9
I think speed limits should be strictly obeyed	59	62	68
I think parking restrictions should be strictly obeyed	44	43	55

The unestablished foreigners are more cautious about the British speed limits and parking restrictions. On the other hand, they have received less exposure to the British campaign against drinking and driving, and an extra 5% of them are willing to condone this.

The same high proportion of British and foreign young people say that it is wrong to sell cigarettes to children under the legal age.

POLITICS

The unestablished foreign young people regard themselves as both more politically active and more left wing than either the British or the established foreign groups. 12% of the unestablished foreigners say that they take an active part in politics, compared with 7% of the British and 5% of the established foreigners. The Conservative party receives considerably more support from the British and established foreigners, while the Labour party receives considerably more support from the unestablished foreigners.

The tendency for the unestablished foreigners to support the Labour party is confirmed by an analysis of their views on specific political issues. 32% of the unestablished foreigners think that the nationalisation of industry is a good thing, compared with 17% of the British and 19% of the established foreigners. 60% of the unestablished foreigners consider that the trade unions have too much power, compared with 74% of the British. 24% of the unestablished foreigners think that private medicine should be abolished, compared with 12% of the British and 15% of the established foreigners.

On the other hand, the foreigners are no more in favour of the abolition of private schools than the British.

Predictably, the foreigners adopt significantly different political attitudes towards Britain itself. The foreign members are much less in support of the notion that immigration into Britain should be restricted. Similarly, they are less concerned to support British industry. Only 4% of the unestablished foreigners say that they would rather buy a British car than one made in another country, compared with 12% of the established foreigners and 21% of the British.

Table 7. 7   Politics

	life %	over 5 yrs%	under 5 yrs%
I have confidence in the policies of the Labour party	14	13	27
I have confidence in the policies of the Conservative party	30	26	13
I have confidence in the policies of the Liberal party	7	7	10
I think immigration into Britain should be restricted	71	46	38
I think the Common Market is a good thing	39	43	57

The foreign members are significantly more in favour of the European Common Market. On the other hand, the foreign members are no less anxious about the influence of multinational corporations. 40% of the British and 43% of the foreigners say that too much economic power is in the hands of multinational corporations.

The six items which invite the respondents to assess the economic remuneration of different jobs presents a particular problem for the foreigners. The foreign young people are less well informed about the salaries received in these jobs, and so they tend to prefer neither to agree nor to disagree with the statements. For example, 45% of the unestablished foreigners say that they are not certain whether nurses are underpaid for the job they do, compared with 26% of the established foreigners and 13% of the British.

SOCIETY

In relationship to a number of issues of social concern, the perceptions of the British and foreign young people are very close. The three groups show a very similar level of concern about the risk of pollution to the environment, the risk of nuclear war, the rate of inflation, the crime rate, the problems of homelessness, the problems of unemployment and the problems produced by the credit card.

The unestablished foreigners show more concern about the moral climate of the world in which they live. 19% more of the unestablished foreigners think that it is becoming too easy to obtain an abortion, and 11% more think that there is too much violence on television. Similarly, 39% of the unestablished foreigners think that it is becoming too easy to obtain a divorce, compared with 25% of the British. 49% of them think that pornography is too readily available, compared with 39% of the British.

Table 7. 8   Society

	life %	over 5 yrs%	under 5 yrs%
I believe that the educational standard of schools is declining	67	69	47
I do not see much future for Britain	21	22	29
I believe that it is becoming too easy to obtain an abortion	19	30	38
I believe that there is too much violence on television	29	31	40
I am concerned about the poverty of the third world	65	77	75

Both the British and the foreigners who have lived in Britain for more than five years show a greater concern that the educational standard of schools is declining and that the health service is becoming more inefficient. Thus, in comparison with the British and the established foreign group, 20% less of the unestablished foreigners have formed the opinion that the educational standard of schools is declining. Similarly, 49% of the unestablished foreigners have formed the opinion that the health service is becoming more inefficient compared with 59% of the established foreigners and 61% of the British young people. It is, however, the unestablished foreigners who tend more to the belief that Britain has not much of a future.

Finally, it is the foreign young people, both those who have lived in England for more than five years and those who have lived there for less than five years, who show the greater concern for the poverty of the third world.

WORK

The unestablished foreigners derive much less satisfaction from their work than those who were either born in Britain or have lived there long enough to become established. Nearly 20% less of the unestablished foreigners say that they are happy in their job, or that they like the people they work with.

In spite of this greater degree of unhappiness at work, the unestablished foreigners are not less committed to their work than the British. The same high proportions (87%) of the British and foreign young people think that it is important to work hard. The same proportions (27%) frequently wish they could change their job. Only a minority of both groups say that they only work for the money or that they would rather go on social security than get a job they do not like doing.

Table 7.9   Work

	life %	over 5 yrs%	under 5 yrs%
I am happy in my job	75	78	59
I like the people I work with	87	83	70
I want to get to the top in my work	79	79	84
I would rather go on social security than get a job I do not like doing	18	17	17

The unestablished foreigners show a significantly higher level of ambition than the other groups: 5% more of them want to get to the top in their work.

LEISURE

The unestablished foreigners tend to find their leisure time less fulfilling than either the British or the established foreign young people. In comparison with these other two groups, 23% more of the unestablished foreigners say that they wish they had more things to do with their leisure time.

The foreigners and the British take an equal interest in the sedentary activities of reading books, watching television and listening to music. The two areas in which their leisure pursuits differ are most probably related to social and cultural factors. The foreigners are less likely to go drinking with their friends in their leisure time. Also, although they are not less likely to watch sport in their leisure time, the foreigners are less likely to take an active part in sport. These are social activities which depend to some extent upon the appropriate friendship networks. Another point of difference in leisure time activity is that the unestablished foreigners are less likely to read a newspaper or listen to the radio or television news. News is much less interesting in a foreign country where much of the cultural background and detail is unfamiliar.

Table 7.10   Leisure

	life %	over 5 yrs%	under 5 yrs%
I wish I had more things to do with my leisure time	30	31	53
I often go drinking with my friends in my leisure time	61	45	36
I read a newspaper nearly every day	73	71	62
I listen to the radio or television news nearly every day	94	94	81
I take an active part in sport	78	70	67

The British and the established foreigners have very similar reasons for joining London Central YMCA. By way of comparison the unestablished foreigners give a lower emphasis to the use of the sports facilities and a greater emphasis to the making of friends. 84% of the unestablished foreigners say that they joined to use the sports facilities compared with 92% of the established foreigners and 94% of the British. On the other hand, 51% of the unestablished foreigners say that they joined in order to make friends, compared with 39% of the British and 38% of the established foreigners.

Table 7. 11 Leisure Facilities

	life %	over 5 yrs%	under 5 yrs%
Facilities preferred by the British members			
Circuit training	21	18	12
Lounge area	47	32	37
Parachuting	12	11	5
Squash courts	55	52	36
Swimming pool	89	84	79
Facilities preferred by the unestablished foreigners			
Basket ball	11	18	35
Film show	30	30	35
Judo	7	10	14
Martial arts	8	13	16
Photographic club	15	15	23
Reading room	14	26	42
Swimming classes	8	11	16
Table tennis	26	35	47
Tennis	19	28	27

Table 7.11 sets out the facilities and activities offered by London Central YMCA to show the differences in preferences between the British and foreign groups. Some very clear differences emerge. For example, the British group shows a much greater interest in squash, and the unestablished foreign group shows a much greater interest in basket ball. The preferences of the established foreign group seem to have moved much closer to the British position.

COUNSELLING

A significant proportion of the unestablished foreigners seem to be desperately unhappy in London. 10% say quite bluntly that they hate London. 18% are convinced that they would not advise a young person to come to London to work or to study, compared with 8% of the British and 10% of the established foreigners.

The unestablished foreigners are much less certain than the other groups that London has a lot to offer the young person. 46% of the foreigners think that the young person has to cope with more risks in London than in other cities, compared with 33% of the British. 32% of the foreigners

92

think that it is all too easy to get mixed up with prostitution in London, compared with 22% of the British. 44% of the foreigners think that it is all too easy to get mixed up with drugs in London, compared with 35% of the British.

Table 7. 12 Counselling

	life %	over 5 yrs%	under 5 yrs%
I hate London	4	3	10
I think that London has a lot more to offer the young person than other cities	58	54	48
I think there should be more counselling facilities for young people in London	59	66	72
I have found it helpful to talk about my problems with a minister of religion	9	10	22
I have found it helpful to talk about my problems with a trained counsellor	9	12	19

The foreigners' perceptions of the risks which young people encounter in London make them significantly more aware of the need for counselling facilities. Moreover, the unestablished foreigners have already derived considerably more help from the caring professions than the other groups. It still remains the case, however, that 20% of the British and 21% of the foreign young people say they would never discuss their problems with a trained counsellor, while 35% of the British and 34% of the foreign young people say they would never discuss their problems with a minister of religion.

8 Social Class

Social class is often determined in social research on the basis of the social grading of occupational status. There are several occupational classification systems in current use, but the most frequently used scale is the five point categorisation proposed by the Office of Population, Censuses and Surveys in 1970 and which is currently used in the analysis of many official statistics. This scale is a classification of occupations (or to be precise of 'unit groups' of occupations) according to 'the general standing within the community of the occupations concerned'.[1]

According to this classification system, professionals, like doctors, accountants, solicitors and clergymen, are assigned to social class one. Semi-professionals, like teachers, social workers, journalists and entertainers are assigned to social class two. Social class three includes bus drivers, clerks, secretaries and electricians. Social class four includes postmen, machine operators, bricklayers and bus conductors. Social class five includes the unskilled manual labourers, porters and messengers.

There are a number of problems involved in applying this type of social grading of occupation to the present sample of 16 - 25 year olds. First, as chapter five has already explored, a substantial proportion of the young people aged 21 and under in the sample are students, and students are not yet located within an occupational structure. Second, the ten year period between the ages of 16 and 25 is an occupationally and socially very mobile time in the young person's life. Third, as explored in chapter seven, a considerable proportion of the sample are foreigners not yet firmly located within the British way of life. Fourth, it is likely that a proportion of the young people living in central London are working at occupational levels inconsistent with the expectations of their social standing, for example accepting short term employment in catering or hotels in order to secure temporary accommodation at the city centre.

Nevertheless, the relationship between social class and the attitudes and values held by young people remain a matter of considerable interest and importance. This chapter attempts to make sense of such an analysis by adopting two necessary strategies. First, it is necessary to omit from the analysis the students and those who are unemployed and for whom there is no data on occupational standing. Second, it is wise to accept a relatively coarse framework for the analysis in order to allow for the difficulty involved in assigning young people of this age to precise social categories on the basis of their occupations. Comparison is, therefore, made only between two groups. The young people holding occupations classified as social classes one or two are assigned to the first group, while the young people holding occupations classified as social classes three, four or five are assigned to the second group. Throughout this chapter these two groups are referred to as the higher social group and the lower social group respectively. Four hundred and fifty five of the young people come within the higher social group, while three hundred and five come within the lower social group.

WELL-BEING

There is a relatively clear relationship between the young people's psychological well-being and their assignment to the higher or lower social group on the basis of the general standing within the community of their occupation. The young people working in occupations in social classes three, four and five tend to enjoy a lower level of psychological well-being than those in social classes one and two.

Table 8.1   Well-being

	Upper %	Lower %
I feel my life has a sense of purpose	74	69
I feel no one knows me	11	16
I often long for someone to turn to for affection	46	55
I often feel depressed	24	31
I am worried that I cannot cope	9	15

Although basically the same proportions from both groups, between 84% and 87%, say that they find life worth living, the young people in the lower social group are less likely to feel that their lives have a sense of purpose. Although basically the same proportions from both groups are well adjusted to life at the city centre, with between 58% and 61% saying that they like to have a lot of people around them and between 41% and 42% saying that they find crowds oppressive, the young people in the lower social groups are more likely to say that they feel lonely, isolated or alienated in the city. Thus, 5% more of the lower social group report that they feel no-one knows them. 9% more of the lower social group often long for someone to turn to for affection. Similarly, 26% of the lower social group say that they often long for someone to turn to for advice, compared with 20% of the higher social group.

A considerably greater proportion of the young people in the lower social group report that they often feel depressed, that is to say 31% compared with 24% from the higher social group. Similarly, 6% more of the young people from the lower social group say that they are worried about their ability to cope. However, inspite of this greater tendency towards personal anxiety and depression, the young people in the lower social group are not significantly more likely to contemplate suicide than those in the higher social group. 17% of the young people in social classes one and two, and 18% of the young people in social classes three, four and five report that they have sometimes considered taking their own lives.

WORRY

Knowledge of the social standing of the young person's occupation does not generally help us to predict the issues which are likely to cause them worry. There are no significant differences in the proportions of young people from the different social groups who worry about their debts, their sex lives, their health, the possibility of a breakdown, the risk of getting cancer or about growing old. Similarly, the same proportions of young people from both social groups, between 62% and 64%, report that they are worried about the world situation.

However, there are two worries which do distinguish significantly between the two social groups. These two worries are concerned with work and relationships. The young people working in occupations within social classes one and two tend to worry more about their work and less about their relationships with other people than those working in occupations within social classes three, four and five. Thus, 47% of the young people in the higher social group say that they often worry about their work, compared with 39% of those in the lower social group. 18% of the young people in the higher social group say that they are worried about their relationships with other people, compared with 25% of those in the lower social group.

VALUES

The most striking feature to emerge from Table 8.2 is the way in which the economic values of the young people in the two social groups differ. The young people working in occupations in social classes three, four and five attach much more importance to money than the young people in the higher social classes. 10% more of the young people in the lower social group say that saving money is important to them; 6% more of them value making money, and 5% more of them value spending money. These differences in economic values are not reflected, however, in the young person's attitude towards home ownership. The same proportions of both social groups, between 73% and 74% consider that it is important for them to own their own house.

Table 8.2   Values

	Upper %	Lower %
Saving money is important to me	68	78
Making money is important to me	64	70
Spending money is important to me	54	59
My work is important to me	92	85
Politics is important to me	51	37

The two different social groups also differ significantly in the value they associate with their work. Although the young people in the lower social group attach more importance to making money, they attach less importance than those in the higher social group to work itself. 7% less of those in the lower social group consider that their work is important to them.

Regarding their social values, the two social groups both attach the same level of importance to moral values and to religion. Where they differ in their social values, however, is in their attitude towards politics. The young people in the higher social group are much more likely to attach importance to politics than the young people in the lower social group.

Regarding their personal values, both of the social groups attach the same importance to their home, their family and their friends. They also attach the same level of importance to their personal appearance. Again, where there is a difference between the two groups is concerning the value placed by the young people on their reputation. The young people from the higher social group value their reputation more highly than the young people from the lower social group. 76% of the young people from social classes one and two say that what people think of them is important to them, compared with 69% of the young people from social classes three, four and five.

SELF IMAGE

None of the seven items in this section on self image are significantly related to the social class variable as it is operationalised in this chapter. The same proportions of young people from both of the social groups admit to feelings of resentment when they don't get their own way, that is to say between 61% and 62%. Between 63% and 65% of both groups admit to sometimes taking advantage of people, and between 80% and 83% of those groups admit the occasional feelings of jealousy. Only 3% of both groups deny ever telling lies and 31% of both groups deny ever having stolen anything. Between 21% and 23% of both groups claim that they have never broken their promise, while between 70% and 71% of both groups say that they are always willing to admit when they make a mistake.

BELIEFS

The earlier section on values has already indicated that there is no significant difference in the proportions of young people in the higher and lower social groups who say that they attach importance to religion. This lack of relationship between social class, as defined by occupational status, and religiosity is confirmed by the present section which concentrates specifically on religious beliefs, practices and attitudes.

To begin with, there is very little difference between the levels of religious belief held by the two groups. 54% of the young people in occupations in social classes one and two claim to believe in God, and so do 55% of those in classes three, four and five. 45% of those in the higher social group accept the central tenet of the Christian faith, namely that Jesus Christ is the Son of God, and so do 48% of those in the lower social group. 42% of the higher social group believe in life after death, and so do 43% of those in the lower social group. The only issue on which there is a significant difference in the level of religious belief displayed by the two social groups is that of reincarnation. 27% of those in the lower social group say that they believe in reincarnation, compared with 21% of those in the higher social group.

Second, social class does not seem to make any difference to the proportions of young people who are actively involved in religious

97

practices. About 6% of both social groups say that they take an active part in church. Almost 19% of both social groups claim to have had contact with a place of worship within the last month, and about 9% of both social groups claim to have read the Bible within the last month. Between 41% and 42% of both social groups claim to have prayed within the last month. Between 28% and 29% of both social groups claim to be practising members of a Christian denomination, while between 4% and 5% of both groups claim to be practising members of other world faiths. Where there is a significant relationship between social class and religious practice is in the denominational affiliation of those young people who claim to be practising members of a Christian church. The Roman Catholic church claims the allegiance of 25% of the practising Christians in the higher social group and 46% of those in the lower social group, while the Church of England claims the allegiance of 54% of the practising Christians in the higher social group and 45% of those in the lower social group.

Third, the attitudes held by the young people towards religion do not seem to be related to social class. Thus, 25% of those in the higher social group dismiss the church as irrelevant for life today, and so do 24% of those in the lower social group. 24% of those in the higher social group dismiss the Bible as irrelevant for life today, and so do 27% of those in the lower social group. At the same time, between 59% and 60% of the two groups maintain that religious education should be taught in schools.

Finally, turning attention away from traditional religious beliefs to the wider area of belief in the supernatural and supraterrestrial, it is demonstrated that the young people in the lower social group are more likely to believe in their horoscope. 20% of the young people in the lower occupational status group say that they believe in their horoscope, compared with 15% of those in the higher occupational status group. On the other hand, there is no difference in the proportions of the two groups, between 55% and 56%, who say that they believe there is intelligent life on other planets.

MORALS

Knowledge of the occupational status of the young respondents is not usually a helpful guide to predicting their moral attitudes. Certainly there are no significant differences in the attitudes of the young people in social classes one and two and those in social classes three, four and five towards matters of sexual ethics. Similar proportions of both groups consider that contraception is wrong (between 2% and 3%), that extra-marital co-habitation is wrong (between 4% and 5%) and that the practise of homosexuality is wrong (between 17% and 18%). Similarly, the two groups hold much the same attitudes towards abortion and euthanasia.

Turning attention to the use of alcohol and drugs, the two social groups hold almost identical views about drunkenness and the use of hard drugs. 27% of the young people in the higher social group think that it is wrong to become drunk, and so do 29% of those in the lower social group. 81% of the young people in the higher social group think that it is wrong to use heroin, and so do 82% of those in the lower social group. Where the attitudes of the two groups do differ significantly is in relationship to the use of the softer drugs. The young people in the higher social group are much more accepting of the use of marijuana than the young people in the lower social group. Thus, 42% of those working in occupations classified as class three, four or five think that it is wrong to use heroin, compared with 31% of those in class one and two occupations.

The only other moral issue on which the views of the two social groups significantly differ is that of war. 65% of those in the lower social group argue that all war is wrong, compared with 59% of those in the higher social group.

LAW

The two different social groups present quite different profiles of themselves when it comes to an analysis of their attitude towards the law. The young people in the higher social group take more seriously honesty on financial issues, like paying fares on public transport and paying customs duties, while the young people in the lower social group take more seriously the strict observation of motoring laws and laws regulating the sale of cigarettes to children. Thus 10% more of the young people in social class one and two occupations refuse to condone travelling without a ticket, and 9% more refuse to condone bringing an extra bottle of spirits through the customs. On the other hand, 7% more of the young people in social class three, four and five occupations argue that parking restrictions should be strictly obeyed, 6% more of them argue that speed limits should be strictly obeyed, and 5% more of them stress that it is wrong to sell cigarettes to children under the legal age.

Table 8.3   Law

	Upper %	Lower %
It is not wrong to travel without a ticket if you are not caught	16	26
There is nothing wrong in bringing an extra bottle of spirits through the customs if you are not caught	39	48
I think speed limits should be strictly obeyed	59	65
I think parking restrictions should be strictly obeyed	43	50
There is nothing wrong in selling cigarettes to children under the legal age	10	5

Given these fundamental differences in the attitudes of the two social groups to the law, it is interesting to note that the two groups agree in their attitude towards tax returns and towards drinking and driving.

POLITICS

The young people working in occupations in social classes one and two are considerably more involved in politics than the young people in classes three, four and five. To begin with, 7% of the young people in the higher social group report that they take an active part in politics, compared with only 4% in the lower social group. Secondly, the young people in the lower social group show more indifference towards the claims of the major political parties. Thus, 40% of the young people in the lower social group have not made up their minds about the policies of the Labour party, compared with 31% of those in the higher social group. 45% of the young people in the lower social group have not made up their minds about the policies of the Conservative party, compared with 38% of those in the higher social group. 53% of the young people in the lower social group have not made up their minds about the policies of the Liberal party, compared with 45% of the young people in the higher social group. On balance, 6% more of the young people in the lower social group are resigned to the conclusion that it makes no difference which political party is in power.

Table 8.4   Politics

	Upper %	Lower %
It makes no difference which political party is in power	27	33
I have confidence in the policies of the Labour party	16	13
I have confidence in the policies of the Conservative party	32	26
I have confidence in the policies of the Liberal party	9	4
I think the Common Market is a good thing	49	35

A consequence of the greater political uncertainty of the young people in the lower social group is that all three of the major political parties derive more positive support from the young people in social class one and two occupations than from those in social class three, four and five occupations. Proportionally speaking, 3% more of the young people in the higher social group have confidence in the policies of the Labour party, 6% more have confidence in the policies of the Conservative party, and 5% more have confidence in the policies of the Liberal party.

When asked for their views on specific political issues, the same trend observed in relationship to the respondents' attitude to the political parties themselves is reproduced. The young people in the lower social class occupations are significantly less sure about their own attitude towards a variety of political issues. 40% of the young people in the lower social group are not sure whether the nationalisation of industry is a good thing or not, compared with 35% of those in the higher social group. 19% of the lower social group are not sure whether private schools should be abolished, compared with 13% of the higher social group. 20% of the lower social group are not sure whether private medicine should be abolished, compared with 15% of the higher social group. 48% of the lower social group are not sure whether there is too much economic power in the hands of multinational corporations, compared with 41% of the higher social group. On the other hand, the young people in the lower social group are not less sure than the young people in the higher social group regarding where they stand on trade unions, immigration, British industry and the Common Market. Moreover, the proportions of the young people who think that the trade unions have too much power, or who think that immigration into Britain should be restricted, or who would give preference to buying British are not significantly related to social class. This means that in fact there is only one political issue embraced by the survey which receives a significantly higher degree of support from one of the two social groups: 14% more of the young people from the higher social group deem the Common Market to be a good thing compared with those from the lower social group.

There are no significant social class differences in the way in which the young people evaluate the pay claims of four of the six groups of workers specified in the survey. 81% of the young people in the higher social group consider that nurses are underpaid for the job they do, and so do 82% of those in the lower social group. 60% of the young people in the higher social group consider that doctors are underpaid for the job they do, and so do 58% of those in the lower social group. 6% of the young people in the higher social group consider that car workers are underpaid for the job they do, and so do 5% of those in the lower social group. 24% of both social groups consider the clergy to be underpaid for the job they do. The two groups of workers which are evaluated differently by the young people in different social class of occupations are policemen and miners. The young people in social class three, four or five occupations are more sympathetic towards both of these groups of workers than the young people in social class one and two occupations. Thus, 60% of the young people in the lower social group consider that policemen are underpaid for the job they do, compared with 55% of those in the higher social group. 33% of the young people in the lower social group consider that miners are underpaid for the job they do, compared with 21% of those in the higher social group.

SOCIETY

The survey data demonstrate that social class is an important variable in understanding the young person's attitude towards issues of social concern. The first point to emerge from table 8.5 is that the young people working in social class three, four and five occupations are more pessimistic about the state of British society. 11% more of those in the lower social group say that they believe that the crime rate is rising. 10% more of those from the lower social group believe that the educational standard of schools is declining. In fact, 26% of the young people in the lower social group conclude that they do not see much future for Britain at all, compared with 21% of those in the higher social group.

Table 8.5   Society

	Upper %	Lower %
I believe that the crime rate is rising	70	81
I believe that the educational standards of schools is declining	63	73
I believe that it is becoming too easy to obtain an abortion	15	27
I believe that it is becoming too easy to obtain a divorce	23	35
I am concerned about the poverty of the third world	69	62

The young people in the lower social group are also more reactionary in relationship to certain social trends. A significantly higher proportion of those in class three, four or five occupations think that it is becoming too easy to obtain an abortion or to get a divorce. Similarly, 52% in social classes three, four and five are unhappy about the consequences of credit card facilities, compared with 42% in social classes one and two. 37% of the young people in the lower social group consider that there is too much violence on television, compared with 30% of those in the higher social group. 50% of the young people in the lower social group believe that pornography is too readily available, compared with 38% of those in the higher social group.

Concern about the issues of inflation, homelessness and nuclear war are not clearly related to social class. 84% of the young people in the higher social group are concerned about the rate of inflation, and so are 83% of those in the lower social group. 79% of the young people in the higher social group are concerned about the people who are homeless and so are 76% of those in the lower social group. 74% of the young people in the higher social group are concerned about the risk of nuclear war, and so are 77% of those in the lower social group. On the other hand, issues like the risk of pollution to the environment, unemployment and the poverty of the third world appear to be taken less seriously by the young people in the lower social group than by those in the higher social group. 7% less of those in the lower social group say that they are concerned about the poverty of the third world. Only 72% of the young people in the lower social group say that they are concerned about the problems of unemployment compared with 77% of those in the higher social group. Similarly, 82% of the young people in the lower social group register concern about the risk of pollution to the environment, compared with 87% of those in the higher social group.

WORK

The young people employed in the higher social class occupations seem to derive more satisfaction from their work than the young people employed in the lower social class occupations. Although the same proportions from both social groups, between 85% and 87%, like the people they work with, 9% more of the young people in the higher social group report that overall they are happy in their work. At the same time, 10% less of the young people in the higher social group feel that they frequently wish they could change their job, while 6% more of them are convinced that they want to get to the top in their work.

Table 8.6   Work

	Upper %	Lower %
I am happy in my job	78	69
I want to get to the top in my work	81	75
Frequently I wish I could change my job	25	35
I only work for the money	15	20
I would rather go on social security than get a job I don't like doing	19	13

Important differences in expectations about job satisfaction are also revealed through the two questions which relate work to money. The young people in the higher social class occupations are less likely to consider that they only work for the money: 15% report this to be the case, compared with 20% from the lower social class occupations. At the same time, 6% more of the young people from the higher social group report that they would rather go on social security than get a job they do not like doing.

LEISURE

Not only are the young people in the lower social group less content than those in the higher social group with their working lives, they are also less content with the way in which they occupy their leisure time. 20% more of the young people in social classes three, four and five than those in social classes one and two wish that they had more things to do with their leisure time.

Table 8.7   Leisure

	Upper %	Lower %
I wish I had more things to do with my leisure time	24	44
I watch some television nearly every day	52	61
I read a newspaper nearly every day	72	74
I listen to the radio or television news nearly every day	94	89
I take an active part in sport	74	75

When it comes to an analysis of the way in which they spend their leisure time, there are no significant differences in the proportions of the young people from the two social groups who read books, listen to music, play sport, watch sport, read newspapers or go drinking with their friends in their leisure time. Where there is a significant difference in leisure time activity between the two groups is in relationship to the proportion of time they spend watching television. 9% more of the young people in the lower social group claim that they watch some television nearly every day. Although the young people in the lower social group are more likely to watch television daily, it is the young people in the higher social group who make a more active attempt to keep up with the news broadcasts either on television or on radio.

Regarding the young people's reasons for joining London Central YMCA, those in the lower social group place a much higher emphasis on the social facilities afforded by the club. 45% of the young people in social class three, four or five occupations say that they joined in order to use the social facilities, compared with 36% of those in social class one or two occupations. 58% in social classes three, four and five joined to meet people, compared with 46% in social classes one and two. 48% of those in social classes three, four and five joined to make friends, compared with 31% in social classes one and two.

There are some interesting relationships between social class and the young person's preferences for the recreational facilities and activities afforded by London Central YMCA. To begin with, the young people from the lower social group tend to indicate an interest in a wider range of activities and facilities than the young people from the higher social group. Those in the lower social group tick on average an interest in 10.6 of the 52 facilities, compared with the 9.3 ticked by those in the higher social group. A number of the facilities appeal to equal proportions of the young people from both social groups. In this category come the audio studio, badminton, bible study, billiards, bridge, camping, the chapel, the chess club, circuit training, climbing, the coffee bar, the craft workshop, the cricket club, the dance classes, the do-it-yourself classes, the Duke of Edinburgh Award scheme, the exhibition facilities, facials and massage, handball, kuk sool won classes, the mountaineering club, newspaper production, the painting and drawing classes, parachuting courses, the photographic club, the reading room, rock climbing, slimnastics courses, slimming classes for ladies, the soccer club, the solarium, the sports hall, the sub-aqua club, the swimming pool, table tennis, the volley ball club and weight training. Thirteen of the other activities and facilities have a greater appeal among young people in the lower social group: these are basketball, disco, film shows, gymnastics, judo, keep fit, the lounge area, martial arts, the sauna, swimming classes, tennis, trampolining classes and yoga classes. By way of contrast only two of the facilities have greater appeal among the young people in the higher social group: these are the dark room and the squash courts.

Table 8.8 Leisure Facilities

	Upper %	Lower %
Facilities preferred by the lower social group:		
Basket ball	9	15
Disco	24	34
Film shows	26	33
Gymnastics	13	25
Judo	5	11
Keep fit	31	42
Lounge area	39	48
Martial arts	5	12
Sauna	47	55
Swimming classes	7	13
Tennis	18	23
Trampolining classes	11	20
Yoga classes	14	20
Facilities preferred by the higher social group:		
Dark room	16	10
Squash courts	57	47

COUNSELLING

The young people in the lower social class occupations perceive a greater need for more counselling facilities for young people in London. Their own experience of living and working in London has tended to convince a greater proportion of the young people in the lower social group that London is a dangerous place in which to live. Thus, in comparison with the young people in the higher social group, 13% more of the young people in the lower social group consider that it is all too easy to get mixed up with prostitution in a place like London, while 10% more consider that it is all too easy to get mixed up with drugs in a place like London. On balance, the young people in the lower social group are not more likely to consider London to be a worse place than other cities, nor are they more likely to advise young people against coming to London to work or to study. They are, however, more inclined to consider that the young people who do come to London are in need of the kind of help that counselling agencies can offer.

Table 8.9   Counselling

	Upper %	Lower %
I think it is all too easy to get mixed up with drugs in a place like London	31	41
I think it is all too easy to get mixed up with prostitution in a place like London	17	30
I think there should be more counselling facilities for young people in London	58	65
I would never discuss my problems with a trained counsellor	21	15
I would never discuss my problems with a minister of religion	36	35

The young people in the lower social group are also more likely themselves to experience the need to talk their problems over with someone. 81% of the young people in the lower social group claim that they experience this need, compared with 75% of the young people in the higher social group. Although they have more need to talk their problems over with other people, the young people in the lower social group are not more likely to have experienced help from talking about their problems with others. The greater need is not matched with a greater assistance. Thus, roughly the same proportions of the young both from both social groups report that they have derived help from discussing their problems with parents and friends, as well as with counsellors and ministers of religion.

Looking to their own possible future needs for counselling, the young people in the lower social group appear to be less reluctant than the young people in the higher social group to turn to a trained counsellor. On the other hand, the same proportions of both social groups report a reluctance to turn to a minister of religion.

NOTES

[1] See Office of Population Censuses and Surveys, Classification of Occupations, HMSO, London 1970. For comment see T.S. Robertson, 'Social class and educational research', Educational Research, 16, 189-197, 1974; and F. Bechhofer 'Occupations' in M. Stacey (Ed.) Comparability in Social Research p.p. 94-122, Heinemann Educational, London 1979.

9 Hostels and Bedsitters

The majority of the young people who belong to London Central YMCA do not live alone. They have some sort of family life on which to draw, occasionally living with their parents or their spouse, or, more often, in a house or flat shared with others. Contrasted with the majority are the minority who live either in bed-sitters or hostels, or in fact by themselves. In the present sample 130 members live in hostels, 56 in bed-sitters and 90 live alone in a house or flat. The objective of this chapters is to explore the differences in the quality of life and attitudes between those who live either alone or in hostels or bed-sitters, and those who share houses or flats with others.

WELL-BEING

Those who live in bed-sitters tend to have a considerably lower level of well-being than the other young people. 8% less of those in bed-sitters say that they find life really worth living. Similarly, 68% of those in bed-sitters say that they feel their life has a sense of purpose, compared with 73% of the others. 71% deny that they feel they are not worth much as a person, compared with 82% of the others. 18% more of those in bed-sitters say that they tend to be lonely. 7% more say they feel no-one knows them. Those in bed-sitters are more likely to feel depressed and to consider taking their own lives.

Table 9.1   Well-being

	S%	A%	H%	B%
I find life really worth living	85	86	85	77
I tend to be a lonely person	21	36	22	39
I feel no one knows me	14	10	13	21
I often feel depressed	27	40	27	32
Sometimes I have considered taking my own life	18	24	20	24

KEY	S%	shared accommodation
	A%	living alone
	H%	hostel
	B%	bed-sitter

106

The young people who live alone in a house or flat say that they find life as worth living as those who share accommodation, and as many of them feel that their lives have a sense of purpose. On the other hand, they feel as lonely as those who live in bed-sitters, and like those who live in bed-sitters their thoughts turn more frequently to suicide than those who live with others. Indeed, they register a higher level of depression even than those in bed-sitters. The point is that they are in so many ways completely isolated from other people. 35% of those who live alone say that they often long to turn to someone for advice, compared with 24% of those who live with others and 24% of those in bed-sitters. 20% of those who live alone are worried that they cannot cope, compared with 12% of those who share accommodation and 11% of those in bed-sitters.

By way of comparison, the hostel dwellers fare much better. The hostel dwellers enjoy as great a degree of well-being as those who share their lives with others in a house or flat.

WORRY

It is those who live alone in a house or flat who exhibit the highest level of worry. They are more worried about their debts, their relationships, their health, and even about the world situation. 5% more of those who live alone are worried that they might have a breakdown. Similarly, 50% of those who live alone are worried about their work, compared with 45% of those who share accommodation or live in bed-sitters and 46% of the hostel dwellers. 32% of those who live alone are worried about growing old, compared with 26% of the rest of the sample.

Those who live in bed-sitters also worry more than those who share accommodation with others, but they worry slightly less than those who live alone. For example, they worry about their debts and health more than those who live with others, but less than those who live alone.

Table 9.2   Worry

	S%	A%	H%	B%
I am worried about the world situation	64	70	60	68
I am worried about my debts	21	30	20	27
I am worried about my relationships with other people	21	28	21	25
I am worried about my health	23	34	26	27
I am worried that I might have a breakdown	9	14	9	14

Once again the hostel dwellers do not differ greatly from those who live in shared accommodation. The picture is beginning to emerge from the data that the hostel is able to simulate the supportive nature of the family environment and provide a much more healthy context for young people than the bed-sitter or single flat.

VALUES

Those who live alone place a much higher investment in their work, the making of money and material possessions. 11% more of those who live alone think that making money is important. 9% more rate their work as important. 78% of those who live alone say that it is important for them to own their own house, compared with 73% of the rest of the sample. Those who live alone also tend to place a lower importance on moral values and religion. 5% less of them consider that moral values are important. 28% say that religion is important to them, compared with 32% of the rest of the sample. More of those who live alone regard having a good time as more important than anything else.

Those who live in bed-sitters tend to value certain aspects of their lives and themselves less highly than the other members. For example, they value both their work and having a good time less highly. Similarly, they are less interested in owning their own house: 68% consider this important, compared with 74% of those who share accommodation. Their self-evaluation is such that they tend to be considerably less concerned about what people think of them. Similarly, only 82% say that their appearance is important to them, compared with 89% of the rest of the sample.

Table 9.3   Values

	S%	A%	H%	B%
My work is important to me	88	97	91	82
Moral values are important to me	81	76	81	81
Making money is important to me	65	76	64	64
What people think of me is important to me	74	70	66	54
Having a good time is more important than anything else	33	39	30	21

Finally, the profile which emerges of the values of the hostel dwellers is closer to that of those in shared accommodation than of those in bed-sitters.

SELF IMAGE

The responses of those who live alone or in hostels to the seven items concerned with self image do not differ significantly from those who live in shared accommodation. These three groups thus seem to differ neither in their levels of self-insight, nor in their personal security and consequent willingness to divulge socially undesirable characteristics about themselves.

Those in bed-sitters record a significantly different score in relationship to three of the seven items in this section. This tends to suggest that they are less secure in themselves than those in shared accommodation. 27% say that they have never broken their promise, compared with 21% in shared accommodation. 41% say that they have never stolen anything, compared with 29% in shared accommodation. Only 52% admit to taking advantage of people, compared with 60% in shared accommodation.

BELIEFS

The only really significant relationship between living accommodation and belief concerns the social aspect of religion. Those who live alone, or in hostels or bed-sitters are more likely to be involved in church. 11% of those in bed-sitters, 7% of the hostel dwellers and 8% of those who live alone claim to take an active part in church, compared with 5% of those who share their accommodation with others. This conclusion is confirmed by an analysis of the proportions of each group who say that they attended church or a place of worship within the last week. 15% of those in bed-sitters, 14% of those in hostels and 11% of those who live alone attended church within the last week, compared with 8% of the others.

Although those who live alone or in hostels or bed-sitters tend to be more actively involved in the social aspect of religion, they do not tend to be more religious in other ways. They neither pray nor read the Bible more frequently. As a group, they do not show any more belief in God, in life after death, or in Jesus Christ as the Son of God.

MORALS

The young people who are accommodated in hostels or bed-sitters tend to be morally more conservative than those who live in shared accommodation or those who live in a house or flat alone. This conservatism may well be associated with the quest for the more protective environment supposedly afforded by hostels and bed-sitters.

Regarding sexual ethics, a larger proportion of those who live in bed-sitters or hostels reject homosexuality, abortion and extra-marital intercourse as wrong. Similarly, 16% of those in bed-sitters and 9% of those in hostels say that it is wrong for an unmarried couple to live together, compared with 4% of those in shared accommodation.

Table 9.4   Morals

	S%	A%	H%	B%
I think it is wrong to have sexual intercourse outside marriage	9	9	12	16
I think the practice of homosexuality is wrong	22	22	35	39
I think abortion is wrong	13	11	20	27
I think it is wrong to use marijuana	35	38	47	54
I think it is wrong to become drunk	30	33	39	38

Those in bed-sitters and hostels are also more conservative than the others regarding their attitudes to alcohol and drugs. More of those in bed-sitters and hostels think that it is wrong to use marijuana or to

to become drunk. Similarly, 87% of those in bed-sitters think it is wrong
to use heroin, compared with 74% of those in shared accommodation.

LAW

There is no significant relationship between the kind of accommodation
occupied by the young people and their attitudes to law.

POLITICS

Those who live in bed-sitters are politically more left-wing than the rest
of the sample. 24% of those in bed-sitters say that they have confidence
in the policies of the Labour party, compared with 16% of those in shared
accommodation, 16% of those who live alone and 15% of those in hostels.
By way of contrast, only 19% of those in bed-sitters say that they have
confidence in the policies of the Conservative party, compared with 26% of
the rest of the sample.

This political tendency is confirmed by an analysis of the responses to the
individual political issues. 25% of those in bed-sitters think that the
nationalisation of industry is a good thing, compared with 20% of the others.
21% of those in bed-sitters think that private schools should be abolished,
compared with 11% of the others. 20% of those in bed-sitters consider
that private medicine should be abolished, compared with 15% of the others.

SOCIETY

The young people who live in bed-sitters seem more detached from many
of the issues that concern contemporary society. 15% less of those in bed-
sitters are concerned about the rate of inflation. 5% less are concerned
about the problems of unemployment. 81% of those in bed-sitters are
concerned about the risk of pollution to the environment, compared with
85% in shared accommodation and 87% of those who live alone. 66% of
those in bed-sitters are concerned about the risk of nuclear war, compared
with 74% of those who live alone or in shared accommodation.

Table 9.5   Society

	S%	A%	H%	B%
I am concerned about the rate of inflation	82	82	81	69
I am concerned about the problems of unemploy- ment	73	78	76	68
I do not see much future for Britain	21	24	26	42
I believe that it is becoming too easy to obtain an abortion	21	20	27	32
I believe that it is becoming too easy to obtain a divorce	28	32	32	36

At the same time, those who live in bed-sitters take a more pessimistic view of certain aspects of British society. About 20% more of those who live in bed-sitters say that they do not see much future for Britain. 77% of those in bed-sitters believe that the crime rate is rising, compared with 73% of those in shared accommodation. Significantly more of those who live in bed-sitters believe that it is becoming too easy to obtain a divorce or an abortion. On a number of other issues, however, like the educational standard of schools, the efficiency of the health service, the availability of pornography, violence on television and the credit card, those who live in bed-sitters do not differ significantly from the rest of the membership.

WORK

The young people who live in bed-sitters seem to derive much less job satisfaction than the rest of the sample. Significantly less of those in bed-sitters say that they are happy in their job or that they like the people they work with. Indeed 18% more of those in bed-sitters agree that they only work for the money. The greater degree of dissatisfaction with their work is also reflected in the fact that 32% of those who live in bed-sitters frequently wish that they could change their job, compared with 26% of those in shared accommodation. On the other hand, although those in bed-sitters enjoy their work less, there is no greater tendency for them to say that they would rather go on social security than get a job they do not like doing.

Table 9.6   Work

	S%	A%	H%	B%
I am happy in my job	72	76	76	65
I like the people I work with	83	88	77	74
I only work for the money	16	16	13	34
I want to get to the top in my work	78	93	82	78
I think it is important to work hard	86	91	85	86

The young people who live alone tend to attach more importance to their work than those in shared accommodation. This is most clearly demonstrated by the question regarding ambition. 15% more of those who live alone want to get to the top in their work, compared with those who live in shared accommodation. Moreover, slightly more of those who live alone say that they are happy in their job and that they like the people they work with. 5% more of those who live alone think that it is important to work hard.

LEISURE

The young people who live in bed-sitters tend to be less happy regarding the way in which they spend their leisure time. 12% more of those in bed-sitters than in shared accommodation wish that they had more things to do with their leisure time. Fewer of those in bed-sitters go drinking with their friends: fewer take an active part in sport. The kind of isolation in which they live in bed-sitters possibly makes it more difficult for them to engage in these kinds of social activities. Possibly as a consequence of the fact that they find it more difficult to make the social contacts needed to participate in some sports, more of those who live in bed-sitters find that they spend their leisure time watching other people engage in sport.

22% less of those in bed-sitters watch some television nearly every day. This may be a reflection on the fact that fewer of them have open access to a television in the houses in which they live, rather than a basic lack of interest. Those who live in bed-sitters read newspapers and listen to the news as often as those in shared accommodation.

Those who live alone are not any less content with their leisure time than those in shared accommodation. They watch television less, possibly again because fewer of them have television in their houses. On the other hand, they watch more sport and read more books. 81% of those who live alone often read books in their leisure time, compared with 74% of those in shared accommodation. Unlike those who live in bed-sitters, those who choose to live alone in a house or flat seem to have as well established networks of friends as those in shared accommodation. They take as active a part in sport as those in shared accommodation and more often go drinking with their friends.

Table 9.7   Leisure

	S%	A%	H%	B%
I wish I had more things to do with my leisure time	34	34	39	46
I watch some television nearly every day	61	53	44	39
I often go drinking with my friends in my leisure time	53	59	50	47
I often watch sport in my leisure time	52	57	53	60
I take an active part in sport	78	78	62	59

Although better off than those in bed-sitters, the hostel dwellers seem to have a less successful experience of their leisure time than those in shared accommodation. The hostel dwellers are more likely to wish that they had more things to do with their leisure time. They watch television less, listen to the news less and read newspapers less. 87% of the hostel dwellers listen to the news nearly every day, compared with 91% of those in shared accommodation. 66% of the hostel dwellers read a newspaper nearly every day, compared with 73% of those in shared accommodation. They take a less active part in sport and are less likely to go drinking with their friends.

Generally those who live in bed-sitters seem also to be less hopeful about the potential of their leisure time. They display a lower level of interest in what London Central YMCA can offer them. 89% of those in bed-sitters say they joined to use the sports facilities, compared with 94% of those in shared accommodation. 34% say they joined to use the social facilities, compared with 42% in shared accommodation. 51% joined to meet people, compared with 54% in shared accommodation. On average those in bed-sitters check an interest in eight of the fifty-two facilities or activities available in London Central YMCA, compared with the eleven checked by those in shared accommodation.

This general lower level of interest gives particular significance to the five activities in which those in bed-sitters show a significantly greater degree of interest than the other members. These activities tend to involve a degree of instruction and are comparatively non-social. 7% of those in bed-sitters are interested in the Bible study, compared with 2% of those in shared accommodation. 20% are interested in the chess club, compared with 9% in shared accommodation. 20% are interested in the martial arts, compared with 11% in shared accommodation. 20% are interested in the swimming classes, compared with 9% in shared accommodation. 25% are interested in yoga classes, compared with 15% in shared accommodation.

COUNSELLING

Those who live in bed-sitters have a much less positive attitude towards London than the other young people. More of those in bed-sitters say that they hate London and that they would not advise a young person to come to London to work or to study. They also tend to believe that London is more full of risks and has less to offer than the other members. 42% of those in bed-sitters agree that London has more to offer the young person than other cities, compared with 56% in shared accommodation and 67% of those who live alone. 40% of those in bed-sitters think that it is all too easy to get mixed up with prostitution in a place like London, compared with 25% of those in shared accommodation.

The young people who live in bed-sitters have had a completely different experience of counselling from the rest of the members. On the one hand, they are people who have received less help in discussing their problems with their close friends or their parents. 21% less of those in bed-sitters have been helped by close friends than is the case among those in shared accommodation. 42% in bed-sitters have been helped by their mother, compared with 61% of the others. 29% in bed-sitters have been helped by their father, compared with 36% of the others. On the other hand, those in bed-sitters have received significantly more help than the others through talking about their problems with a minister of religion.

Willingness to talk about problems with a minister of religion does not seem to be significantly related to type of accommodation. 35% in shared accommodation, 34% in hostels, 32% who live alone and 32% in bed-sitters say that they would never discuss their problems with a minister of religion. On the other hand, those in bed-sitters are more reluctant to talk about their problems with a trained counsellor. 27% in bed-sitters say that they would never discuss their problems with a trained counsellor, compared with 20% of the rest of the members.

Table 9.8   Counselling

	S%	A%	H%	B%
I hate London	5	7	3	14
I would not advise a young person to come to London to work or to study	10	9	11	22
I have found it helpful to talk about my problems with close friends	78	72	78	57
I have found it helpful to talk about my problems with a minister of religion	10	16	16	20
I have found it helpful to talk about my problems with a trained counsellor	10	14	16	13

10 Education

Since the purpose of this chapter is open to misinterpretation, it is necessary to emphasise clearly its itended objectives, scope and limitations. The aim is simply to display as clearly as possible the differences in attitudes and values which exist between young people of different levels of academic achievement. It is unusual for leisure facilities to bring together young people of such diverse educational experience as is the case with London Central YMCA. It is highly constructive, therefore, to use this unique data to examine such issues as what the graduate members and non-graduate members have in common and where their attitudes differ. This analysis helps us to appreciate what is involved in catering for such diverse groups side by side.

This chapter is looking at the difference between groups defined in terms of their academic achievement; it is not attempting to attribute these differences directly to the educational process. The comparison between graduate and non-graduate is inevitably confounded with some of the factors already reviewed. For example, the average age of the graduates tends to be higher.

Academic achievement is defined in this chapter by dividing the sample into four groups, the 186 graduate members, the 294 members who have some A levels or equivalent qualifications, the 399 members who have some O levels or equivalent qualifications, and the 149 members who have none of these qualifications or their equivalents.

WELL-BEING

The academically better qualified tend to enjoy a greater sense of well-being. 89% of the graduates say that they find life really worth living, compared with 83% of the non-graduates. 82% of the graduates say that they like living in England, compared with 72% of the non-graduates. At the other end of the continuum of well-being, the graduates are significantly less likely to have feelings of depression or the anxiety that they cannot cope. On the other hand, as many graduates as non-graduates (19%) say that they have sometimes considered taking their own lives.

The graduates tend to be more introverted than those without academic qualifications. 13% more of the graduates say that they find crowds oppressive. Similarly, only 54% of the graduates say that they like to have a lot of people around them, compared with 64% of those who have O levels. The graduates also feel less isolated than those who have no academic qualifications. 14% less of the graduates feel that no-one knows them. Fewer of the graduates say that they often long for someone to turn to for advice. Similarly, 43% of the graduates say that they often long for someone to turn to for affection, compared with 59% of those who have no qualifications, 50% of those with O levels and 49% of those with A levels.

Table 10.1   Well-being

	none %	O %	A %	degree %
I find crowds oppressive	33	37	37	46
I feel no one knows me	24	14	14	10
I often long for someone to turn to for advice	33	25	26	18
I often feel depressed	34	31	27	19
I am worried that I cannot cope	20	14	12	8

WORRY

There is a clear relationship between academic achievement and the issues regarding which the young people worry. The academically unqualified tend to report significantly more worries about themselves. They are more likely to worry about their health, about growing old or that they might have a breakdown. Interestingly, however, when it comes to the specific problem of cancer, the academically qualified are slightly more concerned than the academically unqualified, in spite of the fact that the unqualified are more worried about their health in general. 37% of the unqualified are worried about their health and 35% of them are worried that they might get cancer. By way of comparison, although only 23% of the academically qualified are worried about their health in a general sense, 39% of them are worried that they might get cancer.

Table 10.2   Worry

	none %	O %	A %	degree %
I am worried about the world situation	55	64	68	73
I am worried about my health	37	22	24	22
I am worried about growing old	37	26	25	23
I am worried that I might have a breakdown	16	9	9	8
I am worried about my sex life	14	12	17	21

There are no significant differences in the levels of worry displayed by the four groups in relationship to their work, their debts or their relationships. However, although the graduates are not more worried about their relationships in general, they are significantly more worried about their sex lives. The graduates are also more likely to report that they are worried about the world situation.

VALUES

The academically better qualified take a more seriously minded approach to life. They value their work more highly. They place a greater value on politics and on moral values. 15% less of the graduates are likely to say that having a good time is more important than anything else.

In the case of religion, there is a curvilinear relationship between academic qualifications and the importance attributed to this area by the young people. Those who hold degrees and those who hold no academic qualifications at all both rate religion as of less importance than those who have some O levels or A levels.

Educational attainment is quite unrelated to the importance attributed by the members to either making money or spending money. It is, however, very significantly related to the importance they attribute to saving money The better educated value the saving of money less highly. 60% of the graduates consider saving money important, compared with 80% of the unqualified, 77% of those with O levels and 66% of those with A levels.

Table 10.3   Values

	none %	O %	A %	degree %
My work is important to me	82	89	90	95
Religion is important to me	26	35	33	25
Politics is important to me	28	45	52	60
Moral values are important to me	69	82	85	83
Having a good time is more important than anything else	40	35	28	25

Home ownership is equally important to those with O levels, A levels and degrees, but it is significantly less important to those who have no qualifications. 75% of O level holders, 77% of A level holders and 75% of the graduates consider that it is important for them to own their own house, compared with 66% of the unqualified.

All four groups give the same high evaluation to their family, their home and their friends. The better qualified tend to value themselves more highly and at the same time they tend to need more the positive evaluation of others. 78% of the graduates say that what people think of them is important to them, compared with 63% of the unqualified and 71% of the A level holders.

SELF IMAGE

The academically better qualified are much more willing to admit to the possession of socially undesirable characteristics. Only one of the seven items in this section fails to distinguish between the various levels of academic qualifications. This is the item about stealing. The same proportion of graduates and non-graduates admit to stealing things.

117

Only 2% of the graduates say that they have never told a lie, compared
with 7% of the unqualified. Similarly, 18% of the graduates say that they
have never broken their promise, compared with 24% of the unqualified.
15% more of the graduates admit to feelings of jealousy. 66% of the
graduates say that they sometimes feel resentful when they do not get
their own way, compared with 50% of the unqualified. 71% of the graduates
admit to having sometimes taken advantage of people, compared with 59% of
the unqualified. 20% less of the graduates consider that they are always
willing to admit when they make a mistake.

Table 10.4   Self Image

	none %	O %	A %	degree %
I have never told a lie	7	5	3	2
Sometimes I have been jealous of others	71	76	75	86
Sometimes I have taken advantage of people	59	58	55	71
I am always willing to admit when I make a mistake	82	66	70	62

Two principal considerations help to explain this relationship between
academic qualifications and self image. It is likely that the academically
better qualified possess a deeper insight into themselves and so they are
more able to recognise the presence of socially undesirable characteristics
in themselves. Second, the academically better qualified may be more
secure in themselves and, therefore, less reluctant to reveal their socially
undesirable characteristics through the questionnaire.

BELIEFS

On almost every account the graduates show a lower level of religious
commitment. Only 45% of the graduates claim to believe in God, compared
with 62% of the unqualified, 61% of those with O levels and 58% of those
with A levels. Between 28% and 29% of all four groups claim to be
agnostics. This leaves 26% of the graduates claiming to be atheists,
compared with 10% of the unqualified, 11% of those with O levels and
13% of those with A levels. Similarly, 74% of the graduates claim not to
be practising members of a religious group, compared with 64% of the
unqualified, 62% of those with O levels and 63% of those with A levels.
The graduates are also less likely to have read the Bible recently or to
have prayed recently. Thus, 24% of the graduates have read the Bible
within the last year, compared with 34% of the non-graduates, while 51%
of the graduates have prayed within the last year, compared with 64% of
the non-graduates. Fewer graduates tend to believe in either life after
death or reincarnation. Fewer graduates believe that Jesus Christ is the
Son of God. Fewer graduates think that religious education should be
taught in schools.

The graduates are more likely to have adopted hostile attitudes towards
the church. 34% of the graduates say that the church seems irrelevant for
life today, compared with 22% of the non-graduates. Similarly, 27% of

the graduates say that the Bible seems irrelevant for life today, compared with 23% of the non-graduates.

In spite of the considerable differences in beliefs and attitudes, the graduate is just as likely to have attended church within the last year. The primary difference between the graduate and the non-graduate seems to be this. More of the graduates seemed to have rationalised their belief structure. That is to say that, although fewer graduates believe in God or consider themselves to belong to a church, those who do so are more likely to put their faith into practice and to be active members of a church and more regular church attenders. Interestingly, the same proportion of graduates and non-graduates (5%) say that they take an active part in church. Conversely, among the non-graduates there is a greater tendency to say that they both believe in God and belong to a church, but at the same time not to put their faith into practice.

Table 10.5   Beliefs

	none %	O %	A %	degree %
I believe that Jesus Christ is the Son of God	59	47	41	33
I believe in life after death	41	46	46	35
I believe in reincarnation	27	28	22	15
I think religious education should be taught in schools	56	62	60	52
I believe in my horoscope	23	23	16	8

Regarding secular beliefs, academic achievement makes no significant difference to the proportion of the young people who believe that there is intelligent life on other planets. 51% of the unqualified, 54% of those with O levels, 52% of those with A levels and 53% of the graduates believe there is intelligent life on other planets. On the other hand, the academically better qualified tend to place significantly less credence in their horoscope.

MORALS

The first noticeable relationship between academic achievement and moral attitudes is that the academically better qualified are significantly more certain where they stand on moral issues. For example, 11% of the graduates respond that they are not certain abour their attitude towards homosexuality, compared with 15% of those with A levels, 20% of those with O levels and 24% of those without academic qualifications.
Similarly, 12% of the graduates have not made up their minds about abortion, compared with 14% of those with A levels, 17% of those with O levels and 24% of those without academic qualifications. 3% of the graduates have not formed an opinion on the issue of contraception, compared with 8% of those with A levels, 11% of those with O levels and 12% of those without academic qualifications.

The second noticeable relationship between academic achievement and moral attitudes is that the academically better qualified are very significantly more likely to adopt a liberal position on moral issues. They are less likely to condemn contraception, extra-marital intercourse, homosexuality, abortion or euthanasia as wrong.

Table 10.6   Morals

	none %	O %	A %	degree %
I disagree that contraception is wrong	84	85	91	95
I disagree that it is wrong for an unmarried couple to live together	86	86	91	93
I disagree that homosexuality is wrong	46	54	59	76
I disagree that abortion is wrong	56	66	76	78
I disagree that euthanasia is wrong	39	45	49	52

The graduates also adopt a more accepting attitude towards alcohol and marijuana. 22% of the graduates think that it is wrong to become drunk, compared with 32% of the non-graduates. 21% of the graduates think it is wrong to use marijuana, compared with 40% of the non-graduates. On the other hand, the graduates tend to adopt a slightly stricter attitude towards heroin. 82% of the graduates think that it is wrong to use heroin, compared with 78% of the non-graduates.

The graduates are slightly less likely than the non-graduates to condone war. 65% of the graduates think that all war is wrong, compared with 60% of the non-graduates.

LAW

The academically unqualified are more likely to condone travelling without a ticket or bringing an extra bottle of spirits through the customs. They are not, however, any more likely to condone the dishonest completion of tax returns. 52% of the graduates and 51% of the academically unqualified considered that tax returns should be filled in with complete honesty.

Regarding their attitude towards the motoring laws, graduates are less likely to respect speed limits and parking restrictions. 17% less of the graduates think that speed limits should be strictly obeyed. Similarly, 44% of the graduates think that parking restrictions should be strictly obeyed, compared with 48% of the non-graduates. On the other hand, fewer of the graduates condone drinking and driving.

There is no significant difference in the proportion of graduates (9%) and non-graduates (8%) who condone the selling of cigarettes to children under the legal age.

Table 10.7   Law

	none %	O %	A %	degree %
It is not wrong to travel without a ticket if you are not caught	27	19	22	17
There is nothing wrong in bringing an extra bottle of spirits through the customs if you are not caught	53	42	40	42
There is nothing wrong with drinking and driving if you can get away with it	8	7	3	2
I think speed limits should be strictly obeyed	66	65	61	49

POLITICS

There is a clear relationship between academic achievement of the young people and their level of interest shown in politics. 14% more of the graduates say that they take an active part in politics than the academically unqualified. Similarly, the academically unqualified are considerably more cynical about politics. 40% of the academically unqualified say that it makes no difference which political party is in power, compared with 25% of those who have O levels or A levels and 24% of the graduates. 60% of the graduates say that they have confidence in the policies of one of the three major political parties, compared with only 33% of the academically unqualified.

Among those who support a political party, the Conservative party clearly receives the greatest support from the O level and A level groups. The Conservatives are also the most favoured party among the academically unqualified as well as the graduate members, although among these two groups the Conservative lead is much smaller.

Table 10.8   Politics

	none %	O %	A %	degree %
I take an active part in politics	2	7	7	16
I have confidence in the policies of the Labour party	14	17	16	20
I have confidence in the policies of the Conservative party	16	30	29	25
I have confidence in the policies of the Liberal party	3	7	7	16
I think immigration into Britain should be restricted	66	65	61	49

Regarding the specific political issues which tend to distinguish between party policies, the graduates emerge as slightly more right wing than the

121

rest of the sample in relationship to the issues of nationalisation and private medicine, but less right wing in relationship to trade unions, private schools and immigration. On the one hand, 53% of the graduates disagree that the nationalisation of industry is a good thing, compared with 40% of the non-graduates. 70% of the graduates disagree that private medicine should be abolished, compared with 65% of the non-graduates. On the other hand, 15% of the graduates think that private schools should be abolished, compared with 10% of the non-graduates. 64% of the graduates think that the trade unions have too much power, compared with 72% of the non-graduates. 17% less of the graduates than the academically unqualified think that immigration into Britain should be restricted.

Regarding the European situation, the graduates are significantly more in favour of the Common Market. 59% of the graduates think that the Common Market is a good thing, compared with 32% of the academically unqualified, 37% of those with 0 levels and 48% of those with A levels.

The graduates and non-graduates have the same evaluation of the pay claims of miners, car workers and nurses. The graduates are less sympathetic towards policemen and doctors. 46% of the graduates think that policemen are underpaid for the job they do, compared with 56% of the non-graduates. 51% of the graduates think that doctors are underpaid for the job they do, compared with 59% of the non-graduates. On the other hand, the graduates are more sympathetic towards the clergy. 27% of the graduates think that the clergy are underpaid for the job they do, compared with 21% of the non-graduates.

SOCIETY

There is a strong relationship between their academic achievement and the way in which young people evaluate issues of social concern. This relationship has two clear dimensions.

First, the academically better qualified are less likely to adopt a pessimistic view of British society, or to subscribe to dogmatic criticisms of contemporary life. 49% of the graduates disagree with the statement 'I do not see much future for Britain', compared with 47% of those with A levels, 37% of those with O levels and 32% of the academically unqualified. The graduates are less critical of the educational standard of schools, they see less danger in credit facilities, they are more accepting of current trends in relationship to divorce, abortion and pornography. 10% less of the graduates consider that they are living in a society in which the crime rate is rising: 64% of the graduates believe that the crime rate is rising, compared with 74% of the non-graduates.

There are two interesting exceptions to this pattern. Although the academically better qualified are less likely to criticise the school system, they are no less likely to criticise the health service. 60% of the graduates believe that the health service is becoming more inefficient, compared with 59% of those with O levels or A levels and 52% of the academically unqualified. Although the academically better qualified are less likely to criticise current trends in pornography, they are more critical of current trends in violence. 37% of the graduates believe that there is too much violence on television, compared with 30% of the non-graduates.

Table 10.9   Society

	none %	O %	A %	degree %
I believe that the educational standard of schools is declining	70	64	61	61
I believe that the credit card encourages careless spending	56	48	42	32
I believe that it is becoming too easy to obtain an abortion	35	29	21	16
I believe that it is becoming too easy to obtain a divorce	40	53	29	18
I believe that pornography is too readily available	49	46	45	29
I am concerned about the risk of pollution to the environment	76	85	86	90
I am concerned about the risk of nuclear war	66	68	76	81
I am concerned about the problems of unemployment	63	71	77	82
I am concerned about the poverty of the third world	58	63	74	79

The second basic trend relating academic achievement with social issues is that the academically better qualified tend to register a greater level of concern for the issues which threaten either the whole of today's society, specific minorities or major sub-groups. The academically better qualified are more concerned about the risk of pollution to the environment, the risk of nuclear war, the problems of unemployment and the poverty of the third world. Similarly, 89% of the graduates say that they are concerned about the rate of inflation, compared with 73% of the academically unqualified. 83% of the graduates are concerned about the people who are homeless, compared with 77% of the academically unqualified.

WORK

Most aspects of the young person's attitude towards work do not seem to be significantly related to academic qualifications. 72% of the academically unqualified and 74% of the graduates say that they are happy in their job. 81% of the academically unqualified and 82% of the graduates like the people they work with. 86% of the graduates and 87% of the non-graduates think it is important to work hard. 81% of the graduates and 80% of the non-graduates want to get to the top in their work.

On the other hand, the proportion of young people who say that they only work for the money is significantly related to academic qualifications. 27% of the academically unqualified say that they only work for the money, compared with 17% of those with O levels, 12% of those with A levels and 12% of the graduate members.

The graduates and the academically unqualified are both more likely than those with O levels or A levels to say that they would rather go on social security than get a job they do not like doing. 16% of those with O levels or A levels agree with this statement, compared with 23% of the academically unqualified and 21% of the graduates.

LEISURE

The satisfactory use of leisure time and academic achievement are closely related. 33% more of the academically unqualified wish they had more things to do with their leisure time than the graduates.

Four leisure pursuits are not related to academic achievement. The same proportions of all four groups listen to music, read newspapers, go drinking and take an active part in sport. On the other hand, the academically better qualified read books more and watch television less. Although the academically better qualified generally watch less television, they take a greater interest in the news broadcasts on both television and radio. The academically better qualified spend less time watching sport, although they have no less interest in taking an active part in sport themselves. The academically better qualified are less content in the spectator role.

Table 10.10   Leisure

	none %	O %	A %	degree %
I listen to the radio or television news nearly every day	87	91	90	95
I often read books in my leisure time	60	73	80	84
I watch some television nearly every day	66	62	52	45
I often watch sport in my leisure time	63	53	47	49
I wish I had more things to do with my leisure time	52	41	28	19

An analysis of the reasons given for joining London Central YMCA indicates that the academically better qualified have less interest in the social facilities of the YMCA than the unqualified. 41% of the graduates say that they joined the YMCA in order to meet people, compared with 48% of those with A levels, 57% of those with O levels and 60% of those without academic qualifications. Similarly, 28% of the graduates say they joined the YMCA in order to make friends, compared with 38% of those with A levels, 47% of those with O levels and 48% of those without academic qualifications. On the other hand, all four groups give a similarly high priority to the use of the sports facilities.

The academically better qualified show an interest in a slightly smaller range of the facilities and activities offered by London Central YMCA than the unqualified. On average, each graduate checks an interest in 9.3 of the 52 options listed in the questionnaire, compared with the 10.0 options checked by those with A levels, the 10.2 options checked by those with O levels and the 10.5 options checked by those without qualifications. Table

10.11 sets out the six facilities and activities preferred by the graduates and the fourteen preferred by the non-graduates. The popularity of the other thirty-two options is not related to academic achievement.

Table 10.11   Leisure facilities

	none %	O %	A %	degree %
Facilities preferred by graduates				
Climbing equipment	2	5	5	8
Dark room	9	12	14	24
Film show	26	35	34	33
Mountaineering club	1	3	5	8
Reading room	14	22	23	22
Squash courts	40	49	53	59
Facilities preferred by non-graduates				
Badminton	52	57	50	45
Basket ball	24	18	16	10
Billiards, snooker, pool	40	35	32	25
Dance classes	38	38	39	26
Disco	38	38	28	19
Facials and massage	27	26	20	14
Gymnastics	32	19	19	12
Judo	14	10	8	4
Kuk sool won classes	10	5	4	1
Martial arts	15	13	8	4
Soccer club	12	9	5	3
Table tennis	36	35	31	25
Trampolining classes	17	14	11	8
Weight training	44	32	27	24

COUNSELLING

The academically better qualified have a more positive approach to London. 6% less of the graduates say that they hate London. 30% less of the graduates think of London as a place in which it is all too easy to get mixed up with drugs or prostitution. 9% more of the graduates think that London has more to offer the young person than other cities. The more positive approach of the academically better qualified to London is also reflected in the fact that they believe there is less need for more counselling facilities for young people in London than is the case among the less well qualified. Thus only 54% of the graduates support the notion that there should be more counselling facilities compared with 63% of those with O or A levels and 67% of the academically unqualified.

The academically better qualified experience as much need as the unqualified to discuss their problems. 75% of the academically unqualified and 77% of the other three groups all agree that from time to time they need to talk their problems over with someone. Although the academically unqualified experience the same need as the other groups to talk about their problems, they seem to have experienced less help from doing so

125

either with their friends or parents. 65% of the academically unqualified say that they have found it helpful to talk about their problems with close friends, compared with 79% of those with some academic qualifications. 50% of the unqualified have found it helpful to talk with their mother, compared with 62% of the other groups. 30% of the unqualified have found it helpful to talk with their father, compared with 36% of the qualified. On the other hand, there is no relationship between academic achievement and either the experience of having derived help from the caring professions, or the openness to approach these professions. 20% of the academically unqualified and 19% of the graduates say that they would never discuss their problems with a trained counsellor. 37% of the academically unqualified and 37% of the graduates say they would never discuss their problems with a minister of religion.

Table 10.12   Counselling

	none %	O %	A %	degree %
I hate London	10	7	4	4
I think it is all too easy to get mixed up with prostitution in a place like London	40	29	24	10
I think it is all too easy to get mixed up with drugs in a place like London	50	38	34	20
I think London has a lot more to offer the young person than other cities	54	55	56	63

11 Anglicans and Catholics

The young people who come into membership of London Central YMCA come from a wide variety of religious and secular backgrounds. Many of the world faiths and Christian denominations are represented in the membership. Unfortunately within the present sample of 1,085 young people, a number of these faith positions are represented by insufficient numbers to make detailed statistical comparisons viable between them all. This chapter proposes to concentrate on the three largest groups, the 687 young people who claim to be practising members of no religious faith, the 118 who claim to be Roman Catholics, and the 132 who claim to be Anglicans.

Within the context of a central London youth organisation of a Christian foundation, this comparison between Anglicans and Catholics is particularly significant. The detailed analysis which follows in this chapter illustrates how the pastoral needs of these two groups of young Christians tend to be quite different. As separate groups, Catholic and Anglican young people tend to represent quite distinct cultural and doctrinal backgrounds. First, the Roman Catholic church tends to offer its young people a more distinctive pattern of beliefs and behaviours. Second, the Anglicans are basically British young people who are already well established in the English way of life: only 8% of the Anglican members came to London directly from abroad. On the other hand, more than half of the Roman Catholic young people are basically strangers to the English way of life: 58% of the Roman Catholic members came to London directly from abroad. By way of comparison, 34% of those who belong to no religious faith had moved to London directly from living in another country.

WELL-BEING

The overall impression is that the Anglican young people enjoy a higher level of well-being than those who do not belong to a church, while the Roman Catholic young people have a lower level of well-being than those who do not belong to a church. Significantly more Anglicans say that they find life really worth living. Similarly, 75% of the Anglicans say that they feel that their life has a sense of purpose, compared with 70% of the unchurched. The Anglicans feel more at home in England:7% more of the Anglicans say that they like living in England, although, interestingly, no less of the Anglicans say that they sometimes think of moving away from England to find better prospects elsewhere.

The Anglicans seem better established socially within a network of friends. 9% less of the Anglicans say that they are lonely. Only 8% of the

Anglicans say that they feel no-one knows them, compared with 17% of the unchurched. Although the Anglicans are less lonely than the others, they no less often feel depressed or seek support from others. Nearly the same proportion of the Anglicans and the unchurched say that they often feel depressed and that they often long for someone to whom to turn to for advice. Similarly, 47% of the Anglicans and 49% of the unchurched say that they often long for someone to turn to for affection. 13% of the Anglicans and 12% of the unchurched say they are worried that they cannot cope. Finally, there is no significant difference in the proportions of the Anglicans and the unchurched who have considered suicide. 20% of the unchurched and 19% of the Anglicans say they have sometimes considered taking their own lives.

Table 11.1   Well-being

	none %	R C %	C of E %
I find life really worth living	83	79	90
I like living in England	73	69	80
I tend to be a lonely person	24	25	15
I often long for someone to turn to for advice	24	33	22
I often feel depressed	28	38	26

The Roman Catholic young people tend to be more susceptible to depression than those who have no church contact, and they experience a greater need to turn to others for support. 10% more of the Roman Catholic young people say that they often feel depressed. 11% more of the Roman Catholic young people say that they often long for someone to whom to turn for advice. Similarly, 56% of the Roman Catholic young people say that they often long for someone to turn to for affection, compared with 49% of those who have no church contact. 18% of the Roman Catholics are worried that they cannot cope, compared with 12% of the unchurched. Slightly less of the Roman Catholics say that they find life really worth living or that they like living in England. In spite of experiencing more depression and being more uncertain about their ability to cope, the Roman Catholic young people are no less likely than the unchurched to feel that their lives have a sense of purpose. Nor are the Roman Catholics any more likely than the unchurched to consider suicide.

These differences in well-being may not necessarily be a direct consequence of denominational affiliation, since a number of other factors, like length of residence in Britain, will tend to confound the differences between the three groups. They are, however, important differences to be borne in mind in assessing the distinct pastoral functions of the Anglican and Roman Catholic churches among their young adherents in the inner city.

WORRY

In relationship to their worries, the Anglicans and the Roman Catholics both differ from the unchurched, but in different ways. The Anglicans worry significantly less about their health and about the possibility of

128

having a breakdown. In spite of this, they worry significantly more that they might get cancer. Similarly, 33% of the Anglicans worry about growing old, compared with 28% of the unchurched and 26% of the Roman Catholics.

The Anglicans worry more about their relationships, although they worry less specifically about their sex lives. 12% of the Anglicans are worried about their sex life, compared with 19% of the Roman Catholics and 16% of the unchurched. The Anglicans worry neither significantly more nor significantly less than the unchurched about their work, their debts or the world situation.

Table 11.2   Worry

	none %	R C %	C of E %
I am worried about the world situation	64	70	61
I am worried about my relationships with other people	23	24	29
I am worried about my health	25	29	17
I am worried that I might have a breakdown	11	9	5
I am worried that I might get cancer	34	31	39

The Roman Catholics are more worried about the world situation and their debts. 6% more are worried about the world situation. 27% are worried about their debts, compared with 21% of the unchurched. The Roman Catholics also tend to be slightly more worried about their health, although they are not more worried about growing old, having a breakdown or getting cancer. The Roman Catholics worry neither significantly more nor significantly less than the unchurched about their work, their relationships, or their sex lives.

VALUES

The major interest in the previous two sections on well-being and worry concerns the way in which Roman Catholics and Anglicans seem to differ more from each other than they individually differ from the unchurched. An analysis of the value structures of the three groups presents a different picture. In the case of values, the Roman Catholics and Anglicans have quite a lot in common. What seems to emerge is a contrast in values between the predominantly Christian young people and the predominantly secular young people, rather than a contrast between one Christian denomination and another. On the issue of values, the Christian young people seem to be more united in spite of differences in cultural, social and racial background.

Regarding their economic values, the Christian and non-Christian members do not place a significantly different level of importance on making money. However, having made their money, they do attribute different levels of importance to saving it and spending it. The non-Christians are significantly more interested in spending their money and the Christians are more interested in saving theirs. Similarly, the Christians show a slightly greater interest in their material future through the possibility of home ownership. 78% of the Roman Catholics and 77% of the Anglicans say that it is important for them to own their own house, compared with 73% of those who are not practising members of any church.

The other three areas in which the Roman Catholics and Anglicans share value emphases in common, and in contrast with the unchurched, are concerned with moral values, politics and religion. 5% more of the Roman Catholics and 7% more of the Anglicans say that moral values are important to them. 8% more of the Roman Catholics and 5% more of the Anglicans say that politics is important to them. As is to be expected, many more of those who claim to be practising members of the Roman Catholic or Anglican churches also claim that religion is important to them. Of greater interest, however, are three other observations. First, a large proportion of the young people who claim allegiance to these two denominations, 45% of the Anglicans and 37% of the Roman Catholics, do not value their religious commitment at all highly. Second, religion is given a greater importance by the Roman Catholics than by the Anglicans. Third, as many as 14% of those who claim not to be practising members of any religious group, Christian or otherwise, still say that religion is important to them. By no means has organised religion a monopoly on the religious interest of the population as a whole.

Table 11.3   Values

	none %	R C %	C of E %
Saving money is important to me	68	78	83
Spending money is important to me	56	51	51
Religion is important to me	14	63	55
Moral values are important to me	79	84	86
Politics is important to me	44	52	49

There are no significant differences in the value attached by the Roman Catholics, Anglicans and unchurched to their work or to their friends, to their appearance or to what others think about them.

Finally, the Anglicans emerge as different from both the Roman Catholics and the unchurched in relationship to two of their basic values. The Anglicans are more home-loving and less fun-loving. 95% of the Anglicans say their home and family are important to them, compared with 89% of the unchurched and 81% of the Roman Catholics. 28% of the Anglicans say that having a good time is more important than anything else, compared with 34% of the unchurched and 34% of the Roman Catholics.

SELF IMAGE

There are just two aspects of self image regarding which there are significant differences among the three groups. Both of these distinguish the two Christian denominations from the unchurched, rather than cause a distinction between the two Christian denominations themselves. The Christians are significantly more willing than the unchurched to admit to breaking their promises, but less willing to admit to theft. Thus, 16% of the Roman Catholics and 17% of the Anglicans claim that they have never broken their promise, compared with 24% of the unchurched. 35% of the Roman Catholics and 38% of the Anglicans claim that they have never stolen anything in their life, compared with 29% of the unchurched. It seems that the Christian young people have been encouraged to practise that kind of self analysis which makes them more aware of personal failures like the breaking of promises. The Christians seem also to have been encouraged more to regard theft as a sin, with the consequence either that they tend to steal less, or that they tend to admit to themselves less that they may have stolen something in the course of their lives.

BELIEFS

An analysis of the religious practices of the three groups draws out some important distinctions regarding the spirituality of the Anglican and Roman Catholic young people. Both the Roman Catholics and the Anglicans attach the same kind of importance to prayer with 53% of the Roman Catholics and 51% of the Anglicans reporting that they had prayed within the last week. The really significant point is that only half of those who regard themselves as practising Christians prayed during the past week, and three-quarters within the last month. This means that one in every four of those who regard themselves as practising Christians understands prayer to be a completely unimportant aspect of religious commitment. Church attendance is seen as more important among those who regard themselves as practising members of the Roman Catholic church than among the Anglicans. More than twice as many of the Roman Catholics (33%) attended church within the last week, in comparison with the Anglicans (14%). Bible reading is regarded more highly by the Anglicans than the Roman Catholics. One Anglican in every ten read the Bible during the last week, compared with one Roman Catholic in every thirty-three. 15% of the Roman Catholics say that they have never read the Bible, compared with only 3% of the Anglicans.

There is a surprisingly high level of religious practice among those who claim to be practising members of no religious group. Within the last month, 30% of those who claim allegiance to no religious group say that they prayed, 7% attended a place of worship and 5% read the Bible. To paraphrase a term from the political arena, these must be the floating worshippers - the young people who are showing a lively interest in and quest after a spirituality of their own, but who have not yet arrived at either a firm commitment to or final rejection of a faith position as represented within either one of the Christian denominations or within one of the world religions.

The Roman Catholic young people are more sure about their religious beliefs than the Anglicans. Only 12% of the Roman Catholics are agnostic about their belief in God and none are atheist, compared with 17% of the Anglicans who are agnostic and 2% who claim to be atheist. 86% of the Roman Catholics are certain about the central doctrine of historic Christianity that Jesus Christ is the Son of God, compared with

77% of the Anglicans. 64% of the Roman Catholics are certain that they believe in life after death, compared with 53% of the Anglicans. Similarly, reincarnation is not a Christian doctrine. 43% of the Roman Catholics are certain that they do not believe in reincarnation, compared with only 28% of the Anglicans. In fact one Anglican in every two does not know whether he believes in reincarnation or not.

Not only do the Roman Catholic young people attend church more regularly than the Anglicans, they also consider themselves to be more actively involved in church and at the same time they criticise the church more. 16% of the Roman Catholics agree that they take an active part in church, compared with 13% of the Anglicans. 17% of the Roman Catholics say that the church is irrelevant for life today, compared with 11% of the Anglicans. The Anglicans both take a less active part in church and also tend to think more that religious education should be taught in schools. 84% of the Anglicans say that religious education should be taught in schools, compared with 74% of the Roman Catholics. Perhaps the Roman Catholics are more willing to accept the notion that religious education is a job not for schools, but for the churches themselves outside the context of compulsory secular schooling.

Table 11.4   Beliefs

	none %	R C %	C of E %
I believe in God	44	88	81
I believe that Jesus Christ is the Son of God	32	86	77
I believe in life after death	35	64	53
I believe that religious education should be taught in schools	47	74	84
The church seems irrelevant for life today	29	14	12
The Bible seems irrelevant for life today	29	17	11

Just as a surprising number of those who claim not to be practising members of any religious group nevertheless attend places of worship, read the Bible and pray, so it is that 44% of this group believe in God, 35% believe in life after death, and 32% believe in Jesus Christ as the Son of God. By way of comparison, only one in five of the unchurched firmly reject belief in these aspects of religious faith. A very large proportion are in fact agnostics who have not yet made up their mind where they stand on these issues. Similarly, less than one-third (29%) of the unchurched dismiss either the Bible or the church as irrelevant for life today. Moreover, 47% of the unchurched still think that religious education should be taught in schools. Although not actively receiving their support, the churches by no means totally lack the goodwill of the unchurched young people in the present sample.

Regarding secular beliefs, the unchurched tend to place more belief in the possibility of life on other planets than the practising members of the church. 56% of the unchurched believe there is intelligent life on other planets, compared with 49% of the Roman Catholics and 50% of the

Anglicans. On the other hand, there is no relationship between church membership and belief in horoscopes. 18% of the unchurched, 18% of the Roman Catholics and 18% of the Anglicans believe in their horoscope.

MORALS

The basic picture to emerge in the area of morality is that the Roman Catholic young people hold more conservative moral attitudes than the unchurched, and that the Anglicans are not significantly different from the unchurched in their moral attitudes.

In the area of sexual ethics, 9% more of the Roman Catholics than the unchurched think that the practise of homosexuality is wrong, while 6% less of the Anglicans agree with this moral judgement. 6% more of the Roman Catholics think that it is wrong to have sexual intercourse outside marriage. Similarly, 9% of the Roman Catholics say that it is wrong for an unmarried couple to live together, compared with 4% of the unchurched and 5% of the Anglicans. It is apparent, however, that the majority of the Roman Catholic young people are adopting a liberal attitude towards both homosexual and heterosexual relationships.

Given the specific teaching of the Roman Catholic church on contra-ception, this is a particularly interesting issue to scrutinise. Only 4% of the Roman Catholic young people agree that contraception is wrong, compared with 2% of the unchurched and 1% of the Anglicans. However, considerably more of the Roman Catholics are uncertain about this issue. The tension in their minds is such that they have not fully arrived at a decision. 18% of the Roman Catholics say that they are uncertain whether contraception is wrong or not, compared with 7% of the unchurched and 5% of the Anglicans. This still means that 78% of the Roman Catholic young people are going against the teaching of their church by denying that contra-ception is wrong.

Table 11.5   Morals

	none %	R C %	C of E %
I think it is wrong to have sexual intercourse outside marriage	8	14	7
I think the practice of homosexuality is wrong	23	32	17
I think abortion is wrong	10	36	7
I think euthanasia is wrong	20	34	21
I think it is wrong to use marijuana	35	46	37

Regarding the sanctity of life, 14% more of the Roman Catholics think that euthansia is wrong and 26% more think that abortion is wrong. Given the particular religious sensitivity of the issue of abortion, this question, like that on contraception, is worth closer scrutiny. Once again a higher proportion of the Roman Catholics seem to be under tension on this issue and opt for the uncertain response. 26% of the Roman Catholics say that they are not certain whether abortion is wrong or not, compared with 17%

of the unchurched and 11% of the Anglicans. Looked at another way, only 38% of the Roman Catholics accept abortion as morally right, compared with 73% of the unchurched and 82% of the Anglicans.

The Anglicans also differ from the unchurched as well as from the Roman Catholics in their attitude to war. The Anglicans are more accepting of war than either the Roman Catholics or the unchurched. 53% of the Anglicans think that all war is wrong, compared with 62% of the unchurched and 71% of the Roman Catholics.

The three groups do not significantly differ in their attitude towards heroin: 79% of the unchurched, 81% of the Roman Catholics and 82% of the Anglicans think that it is wrong to use heroin. The Roman Catholics, however, are more conservative in their attitude towards marijuana and alcohol. 11% more of the Roman Catholics think that it is wrong to use marijuana. 37% of the Roman Catholics think it is wrong to become drunk, compared with 27% of the unchurched and 32% of the Anglicans.

LAW

In relationship to three of the seven questions concerned with law abiding behaviour, the Anglicans emerge as more law abiding than either the Roman Catholics or the unchurched. 36% of the Anglicans say that there is nothing wrong in bringing an extra bottle of spirits through the customs, compared with 46% of the unchurched and 45% of the Roman Catholics. 57% of the Anglicans say that tax returns should be filled in with complete honesty, compared with 53% of the unchurched and 51% of the Roman Catholics. Finally, 66% of the Anglicans say that speed limits should be strictly obeyed, compared with 60% of the others.

POLITICS

The Christian young people, both Roman Catholic and Anglican, are both less sceptical about politics and also take a greater interest in politics. Significantly less of the Christians say that it makes no difference which political party is in power. Similarly, 63% of the Anglicans and 54% of the Roman Catholic members support the policies of one of the major three political parties, compared with 46% of the unchurched.

It is an old jibe that the Church of England should be regarded as the Conservative party at prayer. The present data, however, do nothing to undermine the validity of this jibe. The young Anglican of today seems to be following most definitely in the politically conservative footsteps which have come to be associated with Anglicanism. Nearly half the Anglican young people say that they have confidence in the policies of the Conservative party, compared with about a quarter of the other respondents. By way of contrast, only 8% of the Anglicans have confidence in the policies of the Labour party.

The political conservatism of the young Anglicans is confirmed by their views on specific issues which themselves have party political connotations. Only 11% of the Anglicans consider the nationalisation of industry to be a good thing, compared with 20% of the unchurched and the Roman Catholics. 8% of the Anglicans think that private medicine should be abolished, compared with 17% of the unchurched and 11% of the Roman Catholics. 8% of the Anglicans think that private schools should be abolished, compared with 13% of the unchurched and 8% of the Roman Catholics. 80% of the Anglicans consider that the trade unions have too much power, compared with 69% of the unchurched and 68% of the Roman Catholics. Finally, 12% more of the Anglicans are in favour of restricting immigration into Britain.

It is the Roman Catholics who are most in favour of the Common Market. 55% of the Roman Catholics consider that the Common Market is a good thing, compared with 42% of the unchurched and 41% of the Anglicans.

Table 11.6   Politics

	none %	R C %	C of E %
I think immigration into Britain should be restricted	63	57	75
It makes no difference which political party is in power	29	22	24
I have confidence in the policies of the Labour party	16	20	8
I have confidence in the policies of the Liberal party	8	5	8
I have confidence in the policies of the Conservative party	22	29	47

The different political stances of the three groups also comes through clearly from the way in which they evaluate the pay claims of the six different categories of workers listed in the questionnaire. All three groups closely agree about the situation of the nurses. They fail to agree about the doctors, policemen, car workers, miners or clergy. Doctors are more highly valued by the two Christian groups. 67% of the Anglicans and 62% of the Roman Catholics think that doctors are underpaid for the job they do, compared with 54% of the unchurched. Policemen are more highly valued by the Anglicans. 67% of the Anglicans consider that policemen are underpaid for the job they do, compared with 57% of the Roman Catholics and 51% of the unchurched. Miners and car workers are more highly valued by the Roman Catholics and the unchurched. 7% of the unchurched and 8% of the Roman Catholics consider that car workers are underpaid for the job they do, compared with 1% of the Anglicans. Similarly, 27% of the unchurched and 30% of the Roman Catholics consider that miners are underpaid for the job they do, compared with 19% of the Anglicans. Finally, the clergy are most valued by the Anglicans and, as is to be expected, least valued by the unchurched. 44% of the Anglicans consider the clergy are underpaid for the job they do, compared with 26% of the Roman Catholics and 17% of the unchurched.

SOCIETY

The Christians tend to be more convinced than the unchurched young people that they are living in a declining society. The Christians, both the Anglicans and the Roman Catholics, are more convinced that the crime rate is rising. The Christians are also more inclined to believe that the educational standard of schools is declining. 69% of the Anglicans and 67% of the Roman Catholics believe this to be the case, compared with 62% of the unchurched. On the other hand, the Christians are not more inclined than the unchurched to consider that the health service is becoming more inefficient, nor that the credit card encourages careless spending.

The Roman Catholic young people are more concerned about the changes that are taking place in the moral climate of Britain. 35% more of the Roman Catholics believe that it is becoming too easy to obtain an abortion: 27% more of the Roman Catholics believe that it is becoming too easy to obtain a divorce. 9% more of the Roman Catholics believe that there is too much violence on television. 10% more of the Roman Catholics believe that pornography is too readily available. Although the Anglicans are not more concerned than the unchurched about the ease with which it is possible to obtain an abortion, they share something of the Roman Catholics' greater concern about the issues of divorce, violence on television and the availability of pornography. In spite of sharing these criticisms of contemporary British society, the Anglicans are still basically more hopeful about Britain's future than either the unchurched or the Roman Catholics. Only 20% of the Anglicans say that they do not see much future for Britain, compared with 25% of the Roman Catholics and 25% of the unchurched.

Table 11.7   Society

	none %	R C %	C of E %
I believe that the crime rate is rising	70	82	80
I believe that it is becoming too easy to obtain an abortion	19	54	21
I believe that it is becoming too easy to obtain a divorce	23	50	40
I believe that there is too much violence on television	29	38	43
I believe that pornography is too readily available	39	49	50

The Anglicans, Roman Catholics and unchurched share the same levels of social concern about the risk of pollution to the environment, the risk of nuclear war, and the problems of the homeless. The Anglicans are more concerned about the domestic problems of inflation and unemployment. 89% of the Anglicans are concerned about the rate of inflation, compared with 81% of the unchurched. 78% of the Anglicans are concerned about the problem of unemployment, compared with 73% of the unchurched. The Roman Catholics, on the other hand, are more concerned about the poverty of the third world. 74% of the Roman Catholics are concerned about the poverty of the third world, compared with 67% of the unchurched and 69% of the Anglicans.

WORK

The Anglicans are happier in their work than the unchurched, while the Roman Catholics are less happy. This pattern is also reflected in the fact that 88% of the Anglicans say that they like the people they work with, compared with 83% of the unchurched and 79% of the Roman Catholics. 11% more of the Roman Catholics than either the Anglicans or the unchurched say that frequently they wish they could change their job. Similarly, 21% of the Roman Catholics say that they only work for the money, compared with 16% of the unchurched and 17% of the Anglicans.

In spite of their obviously lower level of job satisfaction, the Roman Catholics have no less ambition in their work than the other members. 81% of the Roman Catholics, 81% of the Anglicans and 79% of the unchurched say that they want to get to the top in their work. The Roman Catholics also share with the Anglicans a greater commitment to hard work. 89% of the Roman Catholics and 93% of the Anglicans think that it is important to work hard, compared with 84% of the unchurched.

Table 11.8   Work

	none %	R C %	C of E %
I am happy in my job	70	64	83
Frequently I wish I could change my job	26	37	26
I like the people I work with	83	79	88
I only work for the money	16	21	17

The proportions of the members who say that they would rather go on social security than get a job they do not like doing is not related to religious affiliation. 18% of the Anglicans, 18% of the Roman Catholics and 18% of the unchurched agree that they would prefer to do this.

LEISURE

It is the Roman Catholic young people who are least content with the way in which they spend their leisure time. 44% of the Roman Catholics wish that they had more things to do with their leisure time, compared with 31% of the Anglicans and 34% of the unchurched. However, the three groups do not differ very greatly in what they say they do with their leisure time. Nearly the same proportions of the Roman Catholics, the Anglicans and the unchurched watch sport and take an active part in sport, read newspapers, read books and listen to music in their leisure time. The three differences in the pattern of leisure time activities concern social drinking, watching television and keeping abreast of news broadcasts. It is the Anglican young people who engage most in social drinking, with 67% of the Anglicans reporting that they often go drinking with their friends in their leisure time, compared with 57% of the Roman Catholics and 52% of the unchurched. Although the Roman Catholics tend to watch more television, the Anglicans tend to take a greater interest in the news broadcasts. Thus, 61% of the Roman Catholics watch some television nearly every day, compared with 56% of the unchurched, while 95% of the Anglicans listen to the radio or television news nearly every day, compared with 89% of the unchurched.

In their reasons for joining London Central YMCA, the Roman Catholic members give less emphasis to the sports facilities and more to their friendship needs. 83% of the Roman Catholics say that they joined to use the sports facilities, compared with 92% of the unchurched. 58% of the Roman Catholics say that they joined to meet people, compared with 48% of the unchurched.

All three groups show an interest in approximately the same number of the fifty-two facilities and activities provided by London Central YMCA and listed in the questionnaire. Nor do the three groups differ very greatly in the specific activities or facilities in which they show interest. The Roman Catholic members are less interested in badminton, the coffee bar, the squash courts and the swimming pool. The Church of England members are less interested in basketball, chess and the dark room. As far as the specifically religious activities of London Central YMCA are concerned, 5% of the Anglicans, 2% of the Roman Catholics and 1% of the unchurched show an interest in Bible study. 9% of the Anglicans, 8% of the Roman Catholics and 1% of the unchurched show an interest in the Chapel.

COUNSELLING

The young person's perceptions of the problems of living in London are not significantly related to religious affiliation. For example, 55% of the Roman Catholics, 58% of the Anglicans and 56% of the unchurched think that London has a lot more to offer young people than other cities. The Roman Catholics are, however, more aware of the need for counselling facilities in London. 70% of the Roman Catholics think that there should be more counselling facilities for young people in London, compared with 61% of the Anglicans and 61% of the unchurched.

Table 11.9   Counselling

	none %	R C %	C of E %
From time to time I feel I need to talk my problems over with someone	73	79	82
I have found it helpful to talk about my problems with a minister of religion	6	21	15
I would never discuss my problems with a trained counsellor	22	19	20
I would never discuss my problems with a minister of religion	41	19	24

The Christians seem to be more aware of a greater need to talk over their problems than the unchurched. 79% of the Roman Catholics and 82% of the Anglicans say that from time to time they feel the need to talk their problems over with someone, compared with 73% of the unchurched.

138

Another significant factor is that the Christians have experienced greater help in discussing their problems with their parents. 66% of the Roman Catholics and 70% of the Anglicans say that they have found it helpful to talk about their problems with their mother, compared with 57% of the unchurched. 39% of the Roman Catholics and 43% of the Anglicans say they have found it helpful to talk about their problems with their father, compared with 32% of the unchurched.

The Roman Catholics are more accustomed than the Anglicans to seeking spiritual counsel from their clergy. This denominational difference is clearly reflected in the data. A higher proportion of the Roman Catholics say that they have found it helpful to talk about their problems with a minister of religion, and a lower proportion of the Roman Catholics say that they would never discuss their problems with a minister of religion. On the other hand, there is no significant difference in the proportions of the Roman Catholics, Anglicans and unchurched who have found it helpful to talk about their problems with a trained counsellor. Nor is any one of these groups significantly more willing than the other two to turn to a trained counsellor in order to discuss their problems.

12 Profiles

The purpose of the previous chapters has been to explore the differences between certain easily recognisable groups of young people – men and women, those in their late teens and those in their early twenties, students and workers, British and foreign, and so on. Beneath all the statistical generalisations in these chapters there remain 1,085 unique individuals. The purpose of this final chapter is to turn attention away from the general to the unique.

The information collected through the questionnaire employed in the survey and completed by the 1,085 young people, upon whom the whole of this study is based, enables us not only to make statistical generalisations, but also to draw up detailed personal profiles for each individual respondent. Space obviously does not permit the presentation of over one thousand detailed personal profiles, but it seems highly desirable to present a sampler of a half a dozen or so cases to indicate something of the depth in which it is possible to encounter the young people from London Central YMCA through the present survey.

The job of generalisation has already been accomplished in the previous chapters. The seven cases presented in this chapter are not claimed to be representative of the young people who come into contact with London Central YMCA. There is possibly no such thing as a typical young member. The few young people chosen for in-depth personal profiles were chosen virtually at random from the last batch of questionnaires included in the total analysis. Ruth is nineteen and married; she is training to be a nurse. Pedro is a twenty-four year old Mexican working as a waiter: he is single. Janet, who is twenty-two and living with her boyfriend, is a student. Mohammad is an eighteen year old Iranian student studying for his GCE's at a residential school. Christine is a twenty-two year old single graduate undertaking post-graduate management training. Michel is a Frenchman beginning his second year of working in London: he is a trained accountant. Ron is a seventeen year old British born youth who is a telex trainee. He is living fifteen miles from the centre of London in shared accomodation. The names attributed to these seven young people are pseudonyms. Moreover, there is no way in which the completed questionnaires can be traced back to the individuals who completed them.

RUTH

Ruth is a nineteen year old trainee nurse at one of the London hospitals. Her parents are both Jamaican, but Ruth herself was born in England and she has lived in the London area all her life. Unlike many of the young

experience of nursing has not been too rewarding. She is not certain whether she is happy in her job or not: nor is she certain that she likes the people she works with. In fact, Ruth frequently wishes she could change her job.

During her leisure time Ruth watches television, listens to music and reads books. She reads a newspaper and listens to the news broadcasts nearly every day. Ruth takes an active part in sport herself, but she does not like the idea of being a spectator watching others engage in sport. She hardly ever goes drinking with friends. At present, Ruth is dissatisfied with her leisure time and wishes that she had more things to do with it. This is probably one of the factors which encouraged her to become a joining member of London Central YMCA. She says that she joined to make use of the sports facilities, to meet people and to make friends. She shows an interest in badminton, dance classes, disco, keep fit, slimming classes, the sports hall, the squash courts and the swimming pool.

Basically Ruth likes living in London. She doesn't believe that London presents the young person with any more risks than other cities. She disagrees strongly that it is too easy to get mixed up with either prostitution or drugs in London. However, she is not too certain whether she would advise young people to come to London to work or to study or not. But she is sure that there should be more counselling facilities for young people in London.

From time to time Ruth experiences the need to talk about her problems with someone. Her past experience indicates that it has been helpful to talk about her problems with her parents, especially her mother. Friends have not been so helpful in this way. Ruth has had no experience of discussing her problems with a minister of religion or a trained counsellor, and she is uncertain whether she would turn to either of them should the need and opportunity arise.

JANET

Janet is a twenty-two year old student. She was born in England, as both her parents were also. This is her second year in London. Before coming to London she lived in a large village in Sussex. Now she lives less than four miles from the city centre in a flat she shares with her boyfriend.

On the whole, Janet is not very happy with her life. She says that she does not find her life really worth living and that her life has no sense of purpose. She is not sure that she likes living in England, but neither is she sure that things would be any better elsewhere. She tends to be a very lonely person, but not so lonely that she feels that absolutely no-one knows her. Her need for affection is met, but she still often longs for someone to turn to for advice. She feels that she is not worth much as a person and she is worried that she cannot cope. She agrees very strongly that she often feels depressed and that she sometimes considers taking her own life.

What worries Janet most is her work. She is also worried about her relationships and about her sex life. She says that the world situation worries her also. On the other hand, Janet does not worry about her health. She has no fears of having a breakdown, or of getting cancer, although she is worried about growing old. Janet has no particular financial worries.

Money is not of much interest to Janet. Neither making money nor
saving money is at all important to her, although she does like spending
money. Although Janet is not interested in owning her own house, she
attaches a high importance to her home. She also says that her family and
friends are important to her, and she places a high value on her work.
Janet takes trouble over her own appearance and it matters to her what
people think about her. On the other hand, she does not attach much
importance to politics or to religion. She is not sure how important moral
values are to her or what importance she gives to seeking pleasure.

The questions about her self image were difficult for Janet to answer.
Generally, she is willing neither to admit to having any socially undesirable
characteristics, nor directly to deny them. She replies cautiously that she
is not certain whether she has ever broken her promise, told a lie or
stolen anything. She is not certain whether she has ever taken advantage of
people or felt resentful when she did not get her own way. In fact, the
only undesirable quality to which Janet readily admits is that sometimes
she has taken advantage of others. Janet says that she is always willing to
admit when she makes a mistake.

Religiously speaking, Janet claims to be an agnostic: she is not certain
whether she believes in God or not. She does not believe in reincarnation,
but she keeps an open mind about the possibility of some form of life
after death. Certainly she does not believe that Jesus Christ is the Son of
God. She has not looked at the Bible for more than five years and it was
over a year ago when she last attended a place of worship. However, she
says that she has prayed within the last month. She is not sure whether
the church is at all relevant for life today, but she feels that the Bible
may have some contemporary relevance. She says that religious education
should not be taught in schools. Janet does not believe that there is
intelligent life on other planets, and she is not sure whether or not to
believe in her horoscope.

Janet disagrees very strongly with the suggestions that extra-marital
intercourse or contraception are wrong. She also disagrees strongly with
the suggestion that it is wrong for an unmarried couple to live together.
On the other hand, Janet thinks that homosexuality is wrong. Janet is in
favour of abortion and euthanasia, but against all war. She does not think
it is wrong either to use marijuana or to become drunk, but she agrees
strongly that it is wrong to use heroin.

Janet's attitude to the law is complex. On the one hand, she thinks that
tax returns should be filled in with complete honesty. On the other hand,
she sees nothing wrong in bringing an extra bottle of spirits through the
customs. She is not sure whether she considers it wrong to try to travel
without a ticket or not. She does not consider it wrong to sell cigarettes
to children under the legal age. As a motorist, Janet disagrees that speed
limits should be strictly obeyed and disagrees strongly with the notion that
parking restrictions should be strictly obeyed. She thinks it is wrong to
drink and to drive.

Janet is very sceptical about politics. She takes no part in politics at all
and she thinks that it does not matter which political party is in power.
She disagrees strongly with Labour party policies: she disagrees with Liberal
party policies, and she is not sure what to make of Conservative party

policies. Beneath this apparent apathy, Janet's political views are quite conservative. She agrees strongly that the trade unions have too much power. She is against the nationalisation of industry and in favour of the preservation of private medicine and private schools. She thinks that immigration into Britain should be restricted. She does not know what to make of the Common Market. She has no desire to support British industry by preferring to buy a home produced car than one made in another country. She does not think that doctors, policemen or car workers are underpaid for the job they do, and she thinks that miners are overpaid. She is not sure whether nurses and clergy are underpaid or not.

Janet is happy with the way in which British society is moving, and she sees a good future ahead for Britain. On her assessment, the educational standard of schools is not declining; the health service is not becoming more inefficient; nor is the crime rate rising. She does not find the moral climate unsatisfactory. She does not consider that it has become too easy to obtain an abortion or to get divorced. She does not believe that pornography is too readily available, but she does believe that there is too much violence on television. Janet is very concerned about the threat to present day civilisation through pollution to the environment and through nuclear war. She is concerned about the problems of inflation and unemployment. She is also concerned about the poverty of the third world. She is not concerned about the problems of homelessness.

Although she worries about her work, Janet says she is basically happy in what she is doing. Certainly she does not wish to change her work for something else, although she is far from certain that she likes the people with whom she works. She thinks it is important to work hard, but is not certain that she really wants to get to the top in her field. Janet thinks a job should be much more than a way of making money, but she says that she would rather get a job she does not like doing than go on social security.

At leisure Janet says that she spends a lot of time reading, listening to music and watching television. She reads a newspaper nearly every day and even more regularly listens to the radio and television news. She often goes drinking with her friends. She does not take an active part in sport and she is even less interested in watching sport. Janet often wishes that she had more things to do with her leisure time. In joining the YMCA, Janet says that her main reason was to use the sports facilities: she gives no priority at all to the social facilities. The ten activities in which she plans to take an interest are the dance classes, facials and massage, film shows, keep fit, sauna, the squash courts, the swimming pool, swimming classes, tennis and yoga classes.

On balance, Janet likes living in London and she says that she would advise other young people to come there to work or to study. As she understands it, London puts in front of the young person neither more risks nor more opportunities than other cities. She disagrees very strongly that it is all too easy for young people to get mixed up with prostitution or drugs in London. She does not see a need for more counselling facilities for young people in London.

From time to time Janet feels the need to talk her problems over with someone, and she finds it helpful to do so with her close friends. She says that she has never been helped by discussing her problems with her parents, with a trained counsellor nor with a minister of religion. She is very open to the idea of approaching a trained counsellor should the need arise, but she is adamant that she would never discuss her problems with a minister of religion.

PEDRO

Pedro is twenty-four years old. He was born in Mexico of Mexican parents. He has been living in England for five years and currently works as a waiter. He is single and lives about seven miles from the centre of London in a house which he shares with a group of other people.

Pedro is basically a happy person. He has been in England long enough to have been able to settle into a satisfactory way of life. He says that he likes living in England and now never thinks of moving away to seek something better elsewhere. Pedro finds his life really worth living and says that it has a sense of purpose. Pedro is an extrovert who fits in well with city life. He does not find crowds oppressive, and he likes to have a lot of people around him. He does not tend to feel lonely in London. He says that he has no cause to doubt his own self worth or to be anxious that he cannot cope with life as it comes. He is the kind of person who finds that the friends he has are able to offer him the support, affection and advice which he needs. He is not particularly bothered about what people think of him. Nor does he take much trouble over his appearance. He rarely feels depressed, and has never considered taking his own life.

Worries do not often trouble Pedro. He rarely worries about his work. Nor does he worry much about money matters and debts. He is not anxious about his mental or physical health. The chances of getting cancer or having a mental breakdown do not cross his mind. He does not give a second thought about growing old. The two things that do worry Pedro are the world situation and his personal relationships with other people. Although worried about relationships, he says he has no reason to worry about his sex life.

Money is not at all important to Pedro. Making money, spending money and saving money are not things to which he gives a high priority. Nevertheless, one day he hopes to own his own house. Pedro's home, family and friends are all important to him. He says that he also sees his work as being important to him. Pedro has little time for religion, but he does attach importance to moral values and politics.

Pedro's self image is perhaps not all that accurate. He says that he has never broken his promise and that he has never stolen anything in his life. He says that he has never taken advantage of people and that he never feels resentment when he does not get his own way. He claims that he is always willing to admit when he makes a mistake. The only two socially undesirable qualities which Pedro sees in himself are that sometimes he tells a lie, and sometimes he is jealous of others.

Religion is of little interest to Pedro. He does not belong to a church. Indeed it is more than five years since he attended a place of worship or prayed by himself. He says that he has never read the Bible. On the other hand, Pedro is not completely hostile towards religion. He believes that both the Bible and the church could have some relevance for life today, although he is convinced that religious education should have no place in the school. Pedro's own theological views are confused. In one breath he says that he does not believe in God, and yet in the next breath he says that he believes that Jesus Christ is the Son of God. He believes in both life after death and reincarnation. Pedro believes that there is intelligent life on other planets, but does not believe in his horoscope. Nor does he think that luck has played an important part in his own life.

Pedro has adopted a liberal attitude to heterosexual ethics. He sees nothing wrong in contraception, extra-marital intercourse or in an unmarried couple living together. He is, however, much more conservative in his views on homosexuality. He thinks that the practice of homosexuality is plainly wrong. Pedro is against all war. He is in favour of abortion and euthanasia. He adopts a conservative position on the issues of drugs and alcohol. He says that it is wrong to use both heroin and marijuana, and that it is wrong to become drunk.

Pedro sees himself as a highly law abiding citizen. He agrees that it is wrong to travel without a ticket or to bring an extra bottle of spirits through the customs. He thinks that tax returns should be filled in with complete honesty. He would never condone the selling of cigarettes to children under the legal age. Pedro is also the perfect motorist. As well as refraining from drinking and driving, he thinks that speed limits and parking restrictions should both be strictly obeyed.

Not only are politics important to Pedro, but he also says that he takes an active part in them. He is sure that it does make a difference which political party is in power, and he knows which party has his own support. Pedro has a lot of confidence in the policies of the Labour party, and none in the Conservative or Liberal parties. His views on specific political issues are also clearly left wing. He thinks that the nationalisation of industry is a good thing, and he supports the trade unions. He thinks that private schools should be abolished, although he is not so sure that it would be a good thing to abolish private medicine as well. Pedro is against placing restrictions on immigration into Britain. He says that he himself would want to support British industry through preferring to buy a British car than one made else- where. He thinks that the Common Market is a good thing. Pedro is sympathetic towards the pay claims of all the workers listed in the question- naire apart from the clergy. He agrees that nurses and doctors, policemen, car workers and miners are all underpaid for the job they do. Clergy he does not see as being underpaid.

Pedro says that he is concerned about all the problems that are likely to confront today's society. He is concerned about the risk of pollution to the environment and the risk of nuclear war. He is also concerned about the problems of inflation, unemployment and homelessness, as well as about the poverty of the third world.

Although Pedro is not himself against abortion, he says that he thinks it is becoming too easy to obtain an abortion in today's world. He also believes that it is becoming too easy to get divorced. In Pedro's view, pornography is now too readily available and there is too much violence on television. As Pedro sees it, he is living in a society in which the crime rate is rising, the credit card is encouraging careless spending, and the health service is becom- ing more inefficient. In spite of all this, Pedro still says that he sees a great future ahead for Britain, and he has some confidence left in the education being provided through the schools.

At work Pedro is happy: he likes being a waiter and he likes the people he works with. He does not wish to change his job. He thinks it is important to work hard, and he says that he wants to get to the top in his work. He says that he works because he likes it, and not just for the money. If he were to lose his job, Pedro says that he would rather get another job which he does not like doing than go on social security.

At leisure Pedro is happy also. He says that he has enough to do with his leisure time. He reads books and listens to music. He reads the newspaper and listens to the radio news nearly every day. He takes an active part in sport and often watches sport as well. He often goes drinking with his friends. The one thing Pedro does not do is watch much television.

Pedro joined London Central YMCA both because he wanted to use the sports facilities and because he hoped to meet people and to make friends. He says that he hopes to make use of fourteen of the fifty two activities or facilities offered by the Club. He is interested in basketball, billiards, the coffee bar, dance classes, discos, gymnastics, judo, keep fit, martial arts, the sauna, the squash courts, the swimming pool, playing table tennis and joining the volleyball club.

London is a good city in Pedro's eyes. He thinks that London has a lot more to offer the young person than other cities, and he does not believe that young people are at special risk in London. He would certainly advise other young people to follow in his footsteps to work or to study in London. Nevertheless, he is aware that there are young casualties in London and he thinks that there should be more counselling facilities for young people in the city.

There are times when Pedro himself feels the need to talk about his problems with someone. In the past he has found it helpful to talk with his parents and close friends, but he has also had recourse to and derived help from a trained counsellor. Although he has never been helped by a minister of religion, Pedro says that he would not be against going to a minister of religion should the need and opportunity arise.

MOHAMMAD

Mohammad is an eighteen year old Iranian student. He has been in the London area for three years at a boarding school where he is studying for some GCE examinations. Before coming to London he says that he was living in a city in Iran.

Mohammad says that he is very happy with his life in England. He likes living in England and he finds his life really worth living. He feels his life has a sense of purpose. In his boarding school he says that he is far from being lonely. He likes to have a lot of people around him. He says that his needs for affection and for advice are both adequately met. He rarely feels depressed. He is not anxious about his ability to cope with life. He has confidence in himself as a person.

There is not much that worries Mohammad. He says that he does not worry about his work, money or relationships. He is not worried about his health or the possibilities of having a breakdown or getting cancer. He is not worried about the world situation. There is just one thing which he says does worry him, and that is his sex life.

Mohammad is not sure what kind of priority he gives to money. As yet he has had no experience of earning his own living. He says he is not sure whether making money, saving money or spending money are important to him or not. Looking to the future, however, he agrees strongly that it is going to be important to him to own his own house. Mohammad says that his appearance is important to him, and it matters to him a great deal what people think of him. His home, family and friends are all very important. Also his work is very important to him. He says that moral values are important to him too. He disagrees with the notion that having a good time is more important than anything else. He is not certain whether religion and politics matter to him or not.

Mohammad presents himself as an ideal and highly respectable young man. He says that he has never broken his promise. He has never told a lie. He is always willing to admit when he makes a mistake. He has never taken advantage of people, felt resentment or been jealous of others. However, he is not quite too good to be true: he admits that it would not be true to say that he has never stolen anything in his life.

Religiously, Mohammad belongs to the Muslim faith, but he does not seem to be a practising believer. It is more than a year since he last attended a place of worship. He says that he has never prayed. He has never read the Bible. Mohammad says that he believes in God, but he is uncertain about where he stands on other religious questions. He is agnostic about re-incarnation, life after death and whether Jesus Christ is the Son of God. He is not sure whether either the Bible or the church have any relevance for life today. Nor can he make up his mind whether religious education should be taught in schools. Mohammad believes that there is intelligent life on other planets, but he is not sure whether to believe in his horoscope or not.

Mohammad says that it is not wrong for an unmarried couple to live together: nor is it wrong to have sexual intercourse outside marriage. He has not made up his mind about contraception, homosexuality or abortion. Nor has he made up his mind whether all war is wrong or not. He believes very strongly that euthanasia is wrong, that it is wrong to use drugs like marijuana as well as heroin, and that it is wrong to become drunk.

As far as the law is concerned, Mohammad sees himself as a very law abiding citizen. He would never drink and drive. Speed limits and parking restrictions are to be strictly obeyed. He says that it is wrong to sell cigarettes to children under the legal age, to travel without a ticket, or to bring an extra bottle of spirits through the customs. Mohammad agrees that tax returns should be filled in with complete honesty.

Mohammad does not know what to make of the British political system. He is not sure whether it makes any difference which political party is in power. He is not certain whether he should have confidence in the policies of the Labour party, the Conservative party or the Liberal party. He says that he does not know whether the nationalisation of industry is a good thing, or whether private medicine should be abolished. He is, however, certainly in favour of the preservation of private schools – after all he is attending one himself. He thinks the trade unions have too much power, and he is certain that immigration into Britain should not be restricted. He says that he has no intention of supporting British industry by giving preference to a British car rather than one made in another country. He says that he does not know whether the Common Market is a good thing

or not. Regarding the six different groups of workers listed in the
questionnaire, Mohammad has fixed ideas on the economic worth of only
one of them. He believes that doctors are underpaid for the job they do.
He is not certain whether nurses, policemen, car workers, miners or clergy
are underpaid or not.

Mohammad has not made up his mind whether there is a future for
Britain or not. On the one hand, he believes that the crime rate is rising
and that the educational standards of schools is declining. On the other
hand, he does not accept that the health service is becoming more
inefficient. Regarding the moral climate of Britain, he agrees very strongly
that pornography is too readily available. He also agrees that it is
becoming too easy to obtain an abortion or to get divorced. He believes
that the credit card encourages careless spending. However, he disagrees
with the proposition that there is too much violence on television.
Mohammad is not concerned about the risk of pollution to the environment
or the risk of nuclear war. He is very concerned about the rate of inflation and also concerned about the problems of homelessness. He says that
he is not sure whether he is concerned or not about the problems of
unemployment and the poverty of the third world.

At school Mohammad says he is happy, and that he likes the people he
studies with. He is an ambitious young man who wants very much to get
to the top and he thinks it is very important to work hard. There is
nothing he would rather be doing at the moment than continuing with his
studies. He disagrees strongly that the only reason to work is for the
money. However, he is not sure that he would rather get a job he did not
like doing than go on social security.

At leisure, Mohammad says that he spends a great deal of time watching
television. He also listens to music. He does not spend much time reading
books and he never goes drinking with his friends. He takes an interest in
reading newspapers and in listening to the radio or television news nearly
every day. Mohammad often watches sport in his leisure time, and even
more frequently he takes an active part in sport. He is very content with
the way in which he spends his leisure time at present.

Mohammad is a new member of London Central YMCA. He says that he
joined the YMCA both to use the sports facilities and to use the social
facilities. He has ticked an interest in fourteen of the activities or
facilities offered by London Central YMCA - namely badminton, basketball,
billiards, circuit training, climbing equipment, keep fit classes, the sauna,
slimnastics courses, the solarium, the squash courts, the swimming pool,
table tennis, tennis and weight training.

Mohammad likes living in London. He disagrees that the young person has
to cope with more risks in London than in other cities. In fact he thinks
that London has a lot more to offer the young person than other cities . He
is not certain whether there is a need for more counselling facilities for
the young in London. He would indeed advise other young people to come
to London to work or to study as he has done.

Problems do not seem to trouble Mohammad very much. He says that he
does not often feel the need to talk about his problems. When he does so,
he has been helped by his friends and by his parents rather than by trained
counsellors or ministers of religion. Looking to the future, if the need

should arise, Mohammad has no doubts about his willingness to approach a trained counsellor, but he is not certain that he would want to approach a minister of religion.

CHRISTINE

Christine is a twenty-two year old graduate who has recently arrived in London to embark on a post-graduate retail management training programme. She is single and lives in a flat which she shares with a number of other people less than a mile from the city centre. Before coming to London Christine lived in a large town in the West Midlands. She was born in England, as both her parents were also.

On the surface, Christine seems well suited to her new life in London. She says that she finds her life really worth living. She likes living in England and never gives a second thought to the possibility of moving elsewhere to find something better. She is an extroverted person who likes to have a lot of people around her and who does not find crowds at all oppressive. She is very rarely lonely. She feels that she is worth quite a lot as a person. She does not rely much on others for advice. She rarely feels depressed, and certainly does not worry about her ability to cope with life. Deeper down, however, there is an emptiness in Christine's life. As she sees it, her life lacks a real sense of purpose. At heart she feels isolated as if no-one really knows her, and she often longs for someone to turn to for affection.

Christine takes life seriously, but she is not given to excessive worry. Her work worries her, but money matters do not cause her worry. Her relationships worry her, but her sex life does not. She is worried about her health and about the risk of getting cancer, but she is not worried about growing old or about the possibilities of having a breakdown. Finally, she sees the world situation as a cause for anxiety.

Money seems to play a very important part in Christine's life. She says that making money is very important to her. Saving money and spending money are also important, but less important than making money. Christine says that it is important to her to own her own house. Christine takes a great deal of trouble over her appearance, and it matters to her a lot what other people think about her. Her home and family are important to her and friends are more important still. Her work is important to her, and so are politics and moral values. She disagrees strongly with the notion that having a good time is more important than anything else. Christine is not sure whether religion is of any importance to her or not.

Christine has a very frank and honest self image of herself. She does not seem to feel the need to pull the wool over her own eyes, or to try to do so over other people's eyes. She admits that sometimes she has broken her promise or told lies, and that she has stolen something in the course of her life. She admits that she has been resentful when she did not get her own way. She says that she is not always willing to admit when she makes a mistake.

Religion does not play much of a part in Christine's life. She is not a practising member of a religious group, but she says that she has attended a place of worship, read the Bible and prayed, all within the last year. In fact Christine would call herself an agnostic. She is not sure whether she believes in God or not. She is uncertain, also, whether she believes in reincarnation, life after death, or in Jesus Christ as the Son of God. On the other hand, Christine is not hostile towards religion. She thinks that both the Bible and the church have some relevance for life today, and she also thinks that religious education should be taught in schools. Christine does not know whether to believe that there is intelligent life on other planets or not, but she is very certain that she does not believe in her horoscope.

On moral issues, Christine has adopted very liberal attitudes right across the board. She disagrees strongly with the suggestion that contraception, extra-marital intercourse, unmarried cohabitation or homosexuality are wrong. She also disagrees strongly with the suggestion that abortion, the use of marijuana or inebriation are wrong. She is slightly less emphatic on the issues of euthanasia and the use of heroin, but she still disagrees that they are wrong. What is morally wrong according to Christine is all war.

Regarding her attitude to the law, Christine assesses each issue on its own merits. She believes that tax returns should be filled in with complete honesty. She believes that it is wrong to travel without a ticket. On the other hand, she considers the customs authorities to be fair game: she sees nothing wrong in bringing an extra bottle of spirits through the customs if you can get away with it. She also finds the law about selling cigarettes to children an unnecessary restriction which it is legitimate to violate. Similarly, as a motorist, Christine sees parking restrictions and speed limits as legitimate laws to break. However, she firmly disagrees with trying to get away with drinking and driving.

Although Christine says that politics are important to her, she does not personally take an active part in politics. She is sure that it does make a difference which political party is in power, but she is not at all sure which party to back herself. She knows that she has no confidence in the policies of the Conservative party, but she cannot make up her mind how to evaluate the policies of the Liberal party or the Labour party. Christine's views on specific political issues are in fact a mixture of left wing and right wing attitudes. She thinks the nationalisation of industry is a good thing, but she rejects the abolition of private schools and private medicine. She thinks immigration into Britain should be restricted and she supports the Common Market. Regarding the worth of the six different groups of workers mentioned in the questionnaire, Christine is not sure whether or not policemen, car workers, miners and clergy are underpaid for the job they do. However, she is certain that nurses are underpaid and that doctors are over-paid.

Christine sees a good future ahead for Britain. She finds no evidence to suggest that British society is in decay. She does not believe that the crime rate is rising, that the educational standard of schools is declining, or that the health service is becoming more inefficient. Nor is Christine discontent with the direction in which the moral climate of Britain is moving. She does not consider that it is becoming too easy to obtain an abortion or to get divorced. In her view, pornography is not too readily available, nor is there too much violence on television. She does not consider that the credit card encourages careless spending.

Christine is alert to the problems which she considers a real threat to today's society. And she says that she is concerned about them. She is concerned about the risk of pollution to the environment and about the risk of nuclear war. She is concerned about the rate of inflation, the problems of unemployment and the people who are homeless. She is also concerned about the poverty of the third world.

At work, Christine is very happy and she likes the people she works with. She thinks it is important to work hard, and she is very ambitious. She really wants to get to the top in her work. At present she is not at all interested in changing her job for something else. Christine seems to need a lot of job satisfaction. She does not work just for the money. In fact she says that she would rather go on social security than get a job she does not like doing.

At leisure, Christine is less content. She wishes that she had more things to do with her leisure time. As it is, she says that she often reads books and listens to music. She does not spend much time watching television. She often goes drinking with her friends. She reads a newspaper nearly every day and listens to the news broadcasts even more regularly. She both takes an active part in sport and watches a lot of sport in her leisure time.

Christine is a joining member of London Central YMCA. She says that she has joined both to use the sports facilities and to use the social facilities. She hopes to meet people and to make friends. She has checked an interest in fourteen of the fifty two activities and facilities offered by London Central YMCA - badminton, the coffee bar, the craft workshop, disco, do-it-yourself classes, film shows, the lounge area, the reading room, the squash courts, the swimming pool, table tennis, tennis and yoga classes.

London is a good place to live in according to Christine. She likes being there herself and she has no reservations about advising other young people to come to work or to study there. She agrees strongly that London has a lot more to offer young people than other cities. She also agrees that young people have to cope with more risks in London than in other cities, although she does not consider that it is all too easy to get mixed up with things like prostitution and drugs in London. She is not sure whether there is a need for more counselling facilities for young people in London or not.

From time to time, Christine recognises the need to talk her problems over with someone. In the past she has found it helpful to talk with her mother, but even more helpful to talk with her father and with close friends. She has also been helped by talking with a trained counsellor, but she seems to have had no experience of seeking help from a minister of religion. Looking to the future, Christine would certainly go back to a trained counsellor if she needed help, and she would not feel reluctant to approach a minister of religion in a similar way.

MICHEL

Michel is a twenty-four year old Frenchman whose work brought him to London two years ago. Before coming to London he lived in a large town in France. He is a qualified accountant working in the area of international monetary exchange. He lives about seven miles from the centre of London in a flat which he shares with his girlfriend.

Michel is an extroverted person. He likes to have a lot of people around him, and he is not bothered by crowds. He has quite a high opinion of himself: he thinks he is worth quite a lot as a person. He does not feel isolated in London. He is not lonely, and he feels that there are people around whom he can say really know him. In fact he says he finds life really worth living and that his life has a sense of purpose.

There is another side to Michel which is not, however, so self-confident. He thinks he may sometimes be depressed and a little worried that he cannot cope. He thinks he may sometimes long for someone to turn to for affection or advice. In fact he is not all that sure that he likes living in England, and he often thinks of moving away to find better prospects elsewhere - perhaps back home in France.

Michel does not like to admit to being a worrier, but he knows that it would not be true to say that he does not worry. Certainly he does not mind admitting that he worries about his work. On the other hand, he is sure that he does not worry about money, about getting cancer or about his sex life. He thinks he may worry from time to time about the world situation, about his relationships with other people, about his health, about growing old or about the chances of having a breakdown - but he is none too sure.

Money is not of much importance to Michel. He says quite plainly that making money and spending money are both unimportant. He gives a higher value to saving money, but he would still say that it was comparatively unimportant to him. One day, however, Michel wants to own his own house.

Michel places a very high value on his home and family, as well as on his friends. It is important to Michel what people think about him. On the other hand, he does not attach much importance to his appearance. Michel says that his work and moral values are both important to him. He disagrees with the idea that having a good time is more important than anything else. He attributes no importance at all to politics, and is not sure whether or not religion is important to him.

Michel seems to have quite an honest self image of himself. He admits that he has told lies and that he sometimes breaks his promise. He does not pretend that he has never stolen anything in his life. He knows that he has sometimes been jealous of others and that sometimes he has taken advantage of people. On the other hand, he says that he is always willing to admit when he makes a mistake and that he never feels resentful when he does not get his own way.

Michel says that he is a practising Roman Catholic. He attended church within the last week and prayed within the last week also, but it is more than five years since he last read the Bible. Although he goes to church, Michel does not consider that he takes an active part in church. Indeed he thinks that the church seems irrelevant for life today, and he cannot make up his mind whether the Bible has any relevance for today or not. At heart Michel is not at all certain about his religious beliefs. He says he is not sure whether he really believes in God or not, although he does not hesitate to say that he believes that Jesus Christ is the Son of God. He knows that he does not believe in the non-Christian doctrine of reincarnation, but he is unsure whether he believes in the Christian doctrine of life after death or not. Michel does not think that religious education should be taught in schools. Michel believes that there is intelligent life on other planets. He is very sure that luck does not play a part in his own life, and he most strongly denies belief in his horoscope.

154

On matters of sexual morality, Michel takes a liberal attitude. He disagrees strongly with the suggestion that contraception, abortion, extra-marital sexual intercourse or unmarried cohabitation are wrong. He also disagrees, although less emphatically, that the practice of homosexuality is wrong. Regarding matters of alcohol and drugs, Michel says that it is wrong to become drunk and that it is wrong to use marijuana. He even more emphatically says that it is wrong to use heroin. Finally, he agrees strongly that all war is wrong and that euthanasia is wrong.

Michel is not at all sure what kind of attitude he really adopts to matters of the law. He says that he is not certain whether he thinks it is wrong to travel without a ticket, or whether there is anything wrong in bringing an extra bottle of spirits through the customs. Nor is he sure whether he thinks that tax returns should be filled in with complete honesty or not. As a motorist, Michel is very sure that it is wrong to drink and to drive, and he thinks that speed limits should be strictly obeyed, but he is not sure what he really thinks about parking restrictions. Michel strongly disapproves of selling cigarettes to children under the legal age.

Politically speaking Michel is a sceptic. He says that politics are of no importance to him and he is very emphatic that he does not take an active part in politics. As far as he is concerned, it makes no difference which political party is in power. He says that he is uncertain whether to have confidence in the policies of the Labour party, the Conservative party or the Liberal party. Nor has he any fixed views on central political issues. He has not made up his mind one way or the other on issues like the nationalisation of industry, the abolition of private medicine, the closure of private schools, the power of the trade unions or questions of immigration.

He is sure, however, that the Common Market is a good thing. He has no intention of supporting British industry by giving preference to a British car over one made elsewhere. Michel has not made up his mind whether doctors, policemen, car workers and miners are underpaid for the job they do or not. On the other hand, he is certain that nurses are underpaid for the job they do, and that clergy are overpaid for their job.

Michel's experience of life in Britain has not convinced him that Britain has much of a future. He believes that the crime rate is rising, that the educational standard of schools is declining and that the health service is becoming more inefficient. On the other hand, he does not find the moral climate of Britain unacceptable. He does not believe that it is becoming too easy to obtain an abortion or to get divorced. He does not consider that the credit card encourages careless spending. Nor does he see any evidence to suggest that there is too much violence on television or that pornography is too readily available. Michel says that he is very concerned about the risk of nuclear war. He is also very concerned about the people who are homeless. He is concerned about the rate of inflation, the problems of unemployment and the poverty of the third world. He does not consider the risk of pollution to the environment as a matter for concern.

Michel likes the people he works with. He is ambitious and he wants to get to the top in his work. Work for Michel is much more than just earning a living: he says that he does not work only for the money. However, he is not really happy in his present job and he frequently wishes he could change it. Michel says that he would rather get a job he does not like doing than go on social security.

As far as his leisure time is concerned, Michel says he is very content. He does not wish that he had more things to do with his leisure time. He says that he does not often read books or listen to music. He does not watch much television, nor does he generally read newspapers or listen to the news. He does not often go drinking with his friends. He neither watches sport nor takes an active part in sport. He says that he is joining the YMCA to use the sports facilities, to meet people and to make friends. He has ticked an interest in only three of the fifty two facilities or activities provided by London Central YMCA: he says that he is interested in badminton, the swimming pool and table tennis.

Michel likes living in London, and he would certainly advise other young people to come to London to work or to study. He is not sure whether London has a lot more to offer young people than other cities. He is sure, however, that the young person has to cope with no more risks in London than elsewhere. Nevertheless, he does believe that there should be more counselling facilities for young people in London.

From time to time Michel feels the need to talk his problems over with someone. He has never found it helpful to talk about his problems with either his mother or his father, but he has found it helpful to talk with close friends. So far, he has received help neither from a minister of religion nor from a trained counsellor. He remains open to the idea of discussing his problems either with a trained counsellor or with a minister of religion should the need arise.

RON

Ron is a seventeen year old youth who was born in England. His father is English and his mother American. Ron left school at sixteen with five CSEs and a few O levels, and he came directly to London as a telex trainee. While at school Ron lived in a small village of less than five hundred people in the south west of England. He now lives in shared accommodation a little over fifteen miles from the centre of London.

At the moment Ron is very happy with his life. He says that he finds life really worth living and that his life has a sense of purpose. He feels that he is worth quite a lot as a person. He does not suffer from feelings of depression, nor does he worry about his ability to cope. He has never had reason to contemplate taking his own life. He likes living in England, and yet often thinks of moving away to find better prospects elsewhere. Ron tends to be an introverted person. He finds crowds oppressive and is not sure that he likes to have a lot of people around him. Although he feels that there are some people who really know him well, Ron still longs for someone to turn to for affection and advice. On the other hand, he does not regard himself as a lonely person.

Ron is not the sort of person who worries much about himself. He disagrees strongly with the suggestions that he might be worried about his work or debts, his relationships with other people or his sex life, his mental or physical health, the risk of getting cancer or the problem of growing old. On the other hand, turning attention away from himself, Ron agrees strongly that he is worried about the world situation.

Money plays a very central part in Ron's life. Making money is very important to him. He also places a high value both on spending his money and on saving it. He is not sure that he wants to invest in the future by buying his own house, nor is he sure that having a good time is more important than anything else. Ron places a very high value on his home and family. Although not as important as his home and family, friends are important to Ron as well. He attaches a great deal of importance to what people think about him and he takes trouble over his appearance. Ron says that his work is very important to him, and he claims to attach a lot of importance to moral values. By way of contrast, Ron has no time for politics at all, and he is not sure whether religion matters to him or not.

Ron's self image shows that he regards himself as a comparatively decent person who has some character defects but not major ones like theft or jealousy. While he agrees that he sometimes tells lies, he denies that he has ever broken his promise and denies very strongly that he has ever stolen anything in his life. While he admits to feelings of resentment when he does not get his own way and sometimes to taking advantage of people, he denies strongly the notion that he has sometimes been jealous of others. Finally, he is not sure whether he is always willing to admit when he makes a mistake or not.

Ron agrees strongly that he believes both in God and in life after death. On the other hand, he has not much time for Christianity or for the church. He has not made up his mind about the person of Jesus Christ, whether he is the Son of God or not. He agrees very strongly that the church seems irrelevant for life today, and he is not sure that the Bible has any relevance for life today either. Ron is not a practising member of any religious group. It is more than a year since he last attended a place of worship, read the Bible or prayed. In spite of all this Ron agrees strongly that religious education should be taught in school. Ron lives in a matter of fact world. He disagrees strongly with the notion that luck plays an important part in his life. He has absolutely no belief in his horoscope. He has no views as to whether there is intelligent life on other planets or not.

At the age of seventeen, Ron has made up his mind that there is nothing wrong in having sexual intercourse outside marriage, or in an unmarried couple living together. On the other hand, he has not made up his mind about the issues of contraception and abortion. He thinks that the practice of homosexuality is very wrong. Ron holds a very conservative attitude towards drugs and alcohol. He agrees strongly that it is wrong to use marijuana as well as heroin, and that it is wrong to become drunk. Ron thinks that all war is wrong, but he does not object to the idea of euthanasia.

Ron sees himself as fundamentally a law abiding citizen. He agrees strongly that tax returns should be filled in with complete honesty and that it is wrong to bring an extra bottle of spirits through the customs. He thinks it is wrong to travel on public transport without a ticket. He disagrees strongly that it is permissible to sell cigarettes to children under the legal age. Regarding motoring laws, Ron disagrees strongly with drinking and driving, but he is not sure whether parking restrictions and speed limits should be strictly obeyed or not.

Ron says that politics is not important to him and that he takes no active part in politics. Nevertheless, Ron holds some very strong political views. He believes that it makes a lot of difference which political party is in power. Personally he says that he has a lot of confidence in the policies of the Conservative party and no confidence at all in the policies

157

of the Labour party or the Liberal party. His attitudes towards specific political issues are also very conservative. He thinks that the trade unions have too much power and that the nationalisation of industry is a very bad thing. He strongly supports both private medicine and private schools. He agrees strongly that immigration into Britain should be restricted, although he would not tend to support British industry by preferring to buy a British car. Ron has not made up his mind whether the Common Market is a good thing or not. He thinks that too much economic power is in the hands of multi-national corporations.

As Ron sees it, nurses, clergymen and policemen are underpaid for the job they do, but he does not feel strongly about their situation. Car workers he considers are overpaid but he does not feel strongly about that either. However, he does feel strongly that both doctors and miners are overpaid for the job they do.

Ron holds some very pessimistic views about life in Britain today. He believes strongly that the crime rate is rising, that the educational standard of schools is declining and that the health service is becoming more inefficient. In short he does not see much future for Britain at all. On matters of social concern, Ron says that he is very concerned about the risk of pollution to the environment, the rate of inflation and also the poverty of the third world. While still registering concern, Ron is less passionately concerned about the problems of unemployment. He says that he is not certain whether he is concerned or not about the issue of home-lessness or the risk of nuclear war. Nor has Ron made up his mind whether or not it is becoming too easy to obtain an abortion or to get a divorce. Ron believes strongly that pornography is too readily available, but disagrees strongly that there is too much violence on television.

Ron believes that it is important to work hard and he really wants to get to the top in his work. However, he is not at all certain that he is happy in his job and he does not like the people with whom he works. Consequently, Ron frequently wishes that he could change his job. In fact, he says that he only keeps working for the money. Ron is emphatic that he would rather have a job that he did not like doing than go on social security.

As far as his leisure time is concerned, Ron very much wishes that he had more things to do. As it is he watches some television nearly every day and he often listens to music. He also reads the newspaper nearly every day, but hardly ever reads books. Ron does not often go drinking with his friends in his leisure time. Ron takes an active part in sport and often watches sport in his leisure time as well. He is a new member to the YMCA and says that he has joined primarily to use the sports facilities, although he hopes to make friends through the YMCA as well. There are just four sporting activities in which Ron has an interest and which he hopes to develop within the YMCA, badminton, soccer, swimming and table tennis. He also shows an interest in the photographic club.

Ron likes living in London. He thinks that London has a lot more to offer young people than other cities. At the same time he believes that young people have to cope with more risks in London than elsewhere. In fact he believes strongly that it is all too easy for a young person to get mixed up with drugs and prostitution in a place like London. Nevertheless, Ron would still advise other young people to come to London to work or to study.

Quite frequently Ron feels that he needs to talk his problems over with someone, and he is convinced that there should be more counselling facilities for young people in London. In the past, Ron has found it helpful to talk with close friends and with his mother, but he has never found it helpful to discuss his problems with his father. He has had no previous experience of talking through his problems with either a trained counsellor or a minister of religion. Looking to the future, Ron is emphatic that he would turn to a trained counsellor should the need and opportunity arise, but that he would never turn to a minister of religion to discuss his problems.

Postscript

Youth in Transit has set out to provide a detailed description of the attitudes and values of the sixteen to twenty-five year old young people working and living in the city centre who become members of London Central YMCA. This descriptive task has been accomplished by organising the research information into twelve key attitudinal areas and by analysing these areas from a variety of perspectives. The attitudinal areas reviewed are well-being, worry, values, self image, beliefs, morals, law, politics, society, work, leisure and counselling. Comparisons have been made between men and women, those in their late teens and those in their early twenties, students and workers, the employed and the unemployed, the British born young person and the foreign resident, the professional and the non-professional worker, those who live alone and those who live with others, the graduate and the non-graduate, the Christian and non-Christian.

The objective throughout the analysis has been to allow the data to speak for themselves, with the result that interpretation and conclusions have been kept to a minimum. It is expected that readers will prefer to make their own interpretations, to draw their own conclusions and to formulate their own priorities for further action. Youth in Transit has provided the data from which informed decisions can emerge and on which appropriate policy can be constructed. Accordingly, I have resisted the temptation to write that closing chapter of conclusions which would both pre-empt the readers' creative work of organisation and interpretation, and provide me with the forum in which to publicise my own intuitive responses to the wealth of information under the guise of an authoritive exegesis of research data.

On the other hand, I do not consider it inappropriate to employ a personal postscript as a way of communicating my own excitement at the richness of the quarry made available to me by the London Central YMCA study. In some senses Youth in Transit has been able only to quarry the surface of some of the rich veins of data. This open seam quarrying has been important because it has made available a large quantity of easily accessible nuggets of information which, in their own right, fuel the fires of debate and heat the furnaces in which policy can be forged. At the same time my enthusiasm and curiosity as a researcher has forced me both to sink deeper exploratory shafts at specific points in the data already viewed from the surface, and also to open new areas for surface exploration. In particular two further studies are under way on the final data base of well over four thousand subjects, aged between sixteen and seventy years.

First, Youth in Transit examines the shape of attitudes and values only

160

as far as the age of twenty-five years. My companion study, Young Adulthood, develops the analysis through the next fourteen years of life up to the age of thirty-nine years. The late twenties and thirties define a period of life comparatively ignored by the social researcher. My new analysis enables me to test whether the trends visible among the sixteen to twenty-five year olds continue or change in later life. To begin with I am able to project the comparison made in Youth in Transit, between late teens and early twenties, into the next two phases of life, the late twenties and the thirties. Then I am able to examine whether the differences between various groups like men and women or the employed and the unemployed, identified among the sixteen to twenty-five year olds, are replicated among the twenty-six to thirty-nine year olds. Not only does this further analysis bring insight into the years of young adulthood, it also brings a deeper perspective against which youth in transit can be integrated and evaluated.

Preliminary analysis of the twenty-six to thirty-nine year olds in the sample showed them to be a very interesting group of men and women. Over eighty per cent of them live within a ten mile radius of the centre of London. They are subject to all the problems and frustrations of inner city life as well as benefiting from the unique experience of access to its attractions. The years of young adulthood embrace a wide variety of perspectives. For some these years are years of fulfilment, success and happiness, while for others they can be a time of accentuated loneliness and a growing sense of failure. London Central YMCA seemed especially to have attracted a group of twenty-six to thirty-nine year olds who might other-wise have been isolated in their inner city life. Forty-two per cent of these members are single and a further ten per cent are divorced and not re-married. Thirty-one per cent live alone in flats, hostels or bed-sitters. Twenty per cent have experienced periods of unemployment during the past two years. Of the foreign members, over fifteen per cent are relative newcomers to London, being resident in England for less than one year at the time of coming into membership. There is represented a wide variety of nationalities, religions and socio-economic status defined by employment.

Second, Youth in Transit has described the views of young people on a wide variety of personal and social issues without being in a position to explore the deeper structure of their attitudes and personalities. I selected the mode of analysis employed in the present study not because I was disinterested in executing more sophisticated statistical and theoretical approaches, but because I considered it to be a worthwhile strategy of analysis in its own right, giving direct access to what young people them-selves are saying. Meanwhile, I have also been actively engaged in exploring the deeper psychometric structure of the data, experimenting in the construction of scaled indices and examining theoretical models through path analysis.

This further analysis has an intrinsic interest and value in the exploration of the structure of the social attitudes and personality, but, in order to give it specific and practical purpose, I am currently applying my theoretical rationale to examination of the psychological correlates of the experience of unemployment. The two empirically derived constructs which have proved to be most useful in the exploration of this relationship are depression and radicalism. By locating the insights already afforded into the psychology of youth unemployment in chapter ten of the present study within the context of the wider literature on personality and social attitudes, these constructs provide a new depth to both the theoretical interest and the practical usefulness of the present data bank.

When London Central YMCA sponsored this research project it was moving into a totally new sphere of operation in the confidence that cooperation between a large voluntary youth organisation and academic research would be mutually enriching and lead to both practical and intellectual benefits. The opportunities for research afforded by London Central YMCA are considerable. At the end of its initial research programme, the association has facilitated the development of the Centymca Attitude Inventory, and the production of the initial volumes in a series exploring a wide range of attitudinal issues. London Central YMCA's confidence was well placed: I very much hope that during the next decades the YMCA will build constructively on the foundations for research which it has now so adequately laid.

Appendix: The Centymca Attitude Inventory

Great Russell Street London WC1B 3NQ
Telephone 01-637 8131
Telex 22683 Cables CENTYMCA

CENTYMCA RESEARCH QUESTIONNAIRE

London Central YMCA wants to be of service to all who use its
facilities. To help them provide a better service they have
asked me to find out about the attitudes and interests of the
members themselves. I can only do this with the members
co-operation. Could you please help me by filling in this
questionnaire?

The questionnaire asks you for your views on a number of
important issues, ranging from the way you like to use your
leisure time to your views on life in general. There are
no "right" or "wrong" answers to these questions. I am
interested in what you really think.

Your responses will be used to produce tables. No one will be
able to pull out your individual answers. Your answers are
strictly confidential. The number at the top of this page is
there simply to help me know who has replied, and it will be torn
off on the day I receive it back.

When you have completed the questionnaire could you please seal
it in the envelope and bring it to Club Reception when you come
to collect your membership card. The envelope will be passed
directly to me and no one else at the YMCA will see your answers.

If you would like to talk with me about the questionnaire please
come to see me in my room on the Upper Club Area, UCA 84.

Thank you for your help.

Yours sincerely,

Dr. Leslie Francis.
Leverhulme Research Fellow.

PART 1

This part of the questionnaire asks for some information about yourself.
Please tick the appropriate boxes.

1. Sex

Male	1	
Female	2	

2. Age

Under 18	1	
18 – 19	2	
20 – 21	3	
22 – 23	4	
24 – 25	5	
26 – 27	6	
28 – 29	7	
30 – 39	8	
40 – 49	9	
50 – 59	10	
60 and over	11	

3. Marital Status

Married	1	
Widowed	2	
Separated/divorced	3	
"Living together"	4	
Single	5	

4. Are you

Self employed	1	
In full time employment	2	
In part time employment	3	
A student (full time, supported by a grant)	4	
A student (full time, self supporting)	5	
A student (full time, on secondment)	6	
Unemployed (seeking a job)	7	
Unemployed (due to ill health)	8	
Unemployed (due to domestic circumstances)	9	
Other (please specify ....)	10	

5. How long have you been unemployed during the last two years

Not at all	1	
Less than 1 month	2	
1 – 2 months	3	
3 – 5 months	4	
6 – 11 months	5	
12 – 17 months	6	
18 months or more	7	

6. What is your average
   take home pay
   (student grant etc)

Per week	or Per month		
Under £30	Under £130	1	
£30 – £40	£130 – £170	2	
£40 – £50	£170 – £220	3	
£50 – £60	£220 – £260	4	
£60 – £70	£260 – £300	5	
£70 – £80	£300 – £350	6	
£80 – £90	£350 – £390	7	
£90 – £100	£390 – £430	8	
£100 – £110	£430 – £480	9	
£110 – £120	£480 – £520	10	
Over £120	Over £520	11	

7. At what age did you leave full
   time education (i.e. from
   school, college, etc.) and
   become ready to take up your
   first full time job

Not yet	1	
16 or under	2	
17	3	
18	4	
19	5	
20	6	
21	7	
22	8	
23	9	
24 or over	10	

8. What
   qualifications
   have you (tick
   as many boxes
   as appropriate)

No qualifications	1	
1 – 4 CSE or equivalent	2	
Five or more CSE	3	
1 – 4 O level or equivalent	4	
5 or more O levels	5	
1 – 2 A levels or equivalent	6	
3 or more A levels	7	
First degree	8	
Higher degree	9	
Professional qualification (specify............................)	10	
Secretarial qualification	11	
Business or commercial qualification	12	

9. Are/were your parents
   separated or divorced

Yes	1	
No	2	

170

10. Where do you live			
At home with your parent(s)	1	
House or flat alone	2	
House or flat shared with your family	3	
House or flat shared with others	4	
Hostel	5	
Hall of Residence	6	
Commune	7	
Bedsit	8	
Other (specify ....)	9	

11. How long have you lived in England			
Less than 1 month	1	
1 - 5 months	2	
6 - 11 months	3	
1 - year	4	
2 - years	5	
3 - years	6	
4 - years	7	
5 years or more	8	
All your life	9	

12. Are you a practising member of a Religious Group (in London or elsewhere)			
None	1	
Roman Catholic	2	
Church of England	3	
Methodist	4	
United Reform	5	
Quaker	6	
Baptist	7	
Hindu	8	
Moslem	9	
Buddhist	10	
Humanist	11	
Other (specify....................)	12	

13. When did you last attend church, synagogue mosque, or other place of worship - apart from occasions like weddings or funerals			
Within the last week	1	
Within the last month	2	
Within the last year	3	
Within the last 5 years	4	
More than 5 years ago	5	
Never	6	

171

14. When did you last pray by yourself

Within the last week	1	
Within the last month	2	
Within the last year	3	
Within the last 5 years	4	
More than 5 years ago	5	
Never	6	

15. When did you last read from the bible by yourself

Within the last week	1	
Within the last month	2	
Within the last year	3	
Within the last 5 years	4	
More than 5 years ago	5	
Never	6	

16. What is your job (please be as precise as possible about the position you hold and the nature of the work you do- eg "medical laboratory technician" not just technician)

....
....
....
....
....
....
....

17. Country where you were born   ....

18. Country where your father was born   ....

19. Country where your mother was born   ....

20. How long have you been working, studying or living in the London area

Less than 1 month	1	
1 - 5 months	2	
6 - 11 months	3	
1 - year	4	
2 - years	5	
3 - years	6	
4 - years	7	
5 years or more	8	
All your life	9	

21. How far do you live from the Centre of London (Oxford Circus)

Less than 1 mile	1
1 - 4 miles	2
5 - 9 miles	3
10 - 14 miles	4
15 - 19 miles	5
20 - 29 miles	6
30 - 39 miles	7
40 miles or more	8

22. Before moving to the London area was your home in

Small village (less than 500 people)	1
Large village	2
Small town (less than 50,000 people)	3
Large town (50,000 - 200,000) or small city	4
Major city centre	5
Major city suburb	6
Always lived in London	7

23. Before moving to the London area was your home in

Northern Ireland (specify County.....................)	1
Scotland (specify County............................)	2
Wales (specify County...............................)	3
England (specify County.............................)	4
Elsewhere (specify Country..........................)	5

24. How long have you been a member of London Central YMCA

New member	1
1 - year	2
2 - years	3
3 - years	4
4 - years	5
5 - years	6
10 years or more	7

25. Why did you seek to join London Central YMCA (tick as many boxes as you please)

To use the sports facilities	1
To use the social facilities	2
To meet people	3
To make friends	4
To get accommodation	5
To help with its work	6
Other (specify ....)	7

173

26.   Which facilities in London Central do you use or plan to use
        (tick as many boxes as you please)

Audio Studio	1		Kuk Sool Won Classes	27	
Badminton	2		Lounge Area	28	
Basket Ball	3		Martial Arts	29	
Bible Study	4		Mountaineering Club	30	
Billiards, Snooker, Pool	5		Painting & Drawing Classes	31	
Bridge	6		Parachuting Courses	32	
Camping Equipment	7		Newspaper Production	33	
Chapel	8		Photographic Club	34	
Chess Club	9		Reading Room	35	
Circuit Training	10		Rock Climbing	36	
Climbing Equipment	11		Sauna	37	
Coffee Bar	12		Slimnastics Courses	38	
Craft Work Shop	13		Slimming Class (Ladies)	39	
Cricket Club(Sports Ground)	14		Soccer Club(Sports Ground)	40	
Dance Classes	15		Solarium	41	
Dark Room	16		Sports Hall	42	
Disco	17		Squash Courts	43	
Do it Yourself Classes	18		Sub-Aqua Club	44	
Duke of Edinburgh Award	19		Swimming Pool	45	
Exhibition Facilities	20		Swimming Classes	46	
Facials and Massage	21		Table Tennis	47	
Film Shows	22		Tennis (Sports Ground)	48	
Gymnastics	23		Trampolining Classes	49	
Hand Ball	24		Volley Ball Club	50	
Judo	25		Weight Training	51	
Keep Fit	26		Yoga Classes	52	

This part of the questionnaire contains a number of sentences. Each sentence is about one specific issue. The sentence looks like this:-

	Agree Strongly	Agree	Not Certain	Disagree	Disagree Strongly
1. I enjoyed my time at school	AS	A	NC	D	DS

AS means I Agree Strongly

A means I Agree

NC means I am Not Certain

D means I Disagree

DS means I Disagree Strongly

Read the sentence carefully and think, "Do I agree with it?"

If you Agree Strongly, put a ring round ...	(AS)	A	NC	D	DS
If you Agree, put a ring round	AS	(A)	NC	D	DS
If you are Not Certain, put a ring round ...	AS	A	(NC)	D	DS
If you Disagree, put a ring round	AS	A	NC	(D)	DS
If you Disagree Strongly, put a ring round ...	AS	A	NC	D	(DS)

Now please answer the next question

2. I like watching sport on the television ...	AS	A	NC	D	DS

Please answer the questions as you really think. Your answers will be confidential.

And now please turn over and go on with the rest of the sentences.

YMCAAI1/LJF78

	Agree Strongly	Agree	Not Certain	Disagree	Disagree Strongly
I listen to the radio or television news nearly every day	AS	A	NC	D	DS
I am concerned about the poverty of the third world	AS	A	NC	D	DS
Frequently I wish I could change my job	AS	A	NC	D	DS
I like living in England	AS	A	NC	D	DS
I believe in reincarnation	AS	A	NC	D	DS
Politics is important to me	AS	A	NC	D	DS
I believe that the educational standard of schools is declining	AS	A	NC	D	DS
I take an active part in sport	AS	A	NC	D	DS
I have confidence in the policies of the Labour party	AS	A	NC	D	DS
I often feel depressed	AS	A	NC	D	DS
I think all war is wrong	AS	A	NC	D	DS
I like the people I work with	AS	A	NC	D	DS
I have never told a lie	AS	A	NC	D	DS
I believe that Jesus Christ is the Son of God	AS	A	NC	D	DS

YMCAAI1/LJF78

	Agree Strongly	Agree	Not Certain	Disagree	Disagree Strongly
I believe that it is becoming too easy to obtain an abortion	AS	A	NC	D	DS
I am worried about growing old	AS	A	NC	D	DS
I don't see much future for Britain	AS	A	NC	D	DS
There is nothing wrong in selling cigarettes to children under the legal age	AS	A	NC	D	DS
I would never discuss my problems with a trained counsellor	AS	A	NC	D	DS
I only work for the money	AS	A	NC	D	DS
Friends are important to me	AS	A	NC	D	DS
I wouldn't advise a young person to come to London to work or to study	AS	A	NC	D	DS
I am worried about my relationships with other people	AS	A	NC	D	DS
I believe that the credit card encourages careless spending	AS	A	NC	D	DS
I am worried about my health	AS	A	NC	D	DS
I believe that the crime rate is rising	AS	A	NC	D	DS
I think contraception is wrong	AS	A	NC	D	DS
The young person has to cope with more risks in London than in other cities	AS	A	NC	D	DS

YMCAAI1/LJF78

	Agree Strongly	Agree	Not Certain	Disagree	Disagree Strongly
I have found it helpful to talk about my problems with close friends	AS	A	NC	D	DS
Religion is important to me	AS	A	NC	D	DS
I like to do things that are a little frightening	AS	A	NC	D	DS
I think parking restrictions should be strictly obeyed	AS	A	NC	D	DS
I think private schools should be abolished ...	AS	A	NC	D	DS
Moral values are important to me	AS	A	NC	D	DS
I watch some television nearly every day ...	AS	A	NC	D	DS
I think doctors are underpaid for the job they do	AS	A	NC	D	DS
Saving money is important to me	AS	A	NC	D	DS
I believe that pornography is too readily available	AS	A	NC	D	DS
I think euthanasia (mercy killing) is wrong ...	AS	A	NC	D	DS
I often read books in my leisure time	AS	A	NC	D	DS
I feel I am not worth much as a person	AS	A	NC	D	DS
I think it is wrong to have sexual intercourse outside marriage	AS	A	NC	D	DS

YMCAAI1/LJF78

	Agree Strongly	Agree	Not Certain	Disagree	Disagree Strongly
I think abortion is wrong	AS	A	NC	D	DS
I am concerned about people who are homeless ...	AS	A	NC	D	DS
The bible seems irrelevant for life today	AS	A	NC	D	DS
I am worried that I cannot cope	AS	A	NC	D	DS
I wish I had more things to do with my leisure time	AS	A	NC	D	DS
I think policemen are underpaid for the job they do	AS	A	NC	D	DS
I often listen to music in my leisure time ...	AS	A	NC	D	DS
I am concerned about the risk of pollution to the environment	AS	A	NC	D	DS
I often go drinking with friends in my leisure time	AS	A	NC	D	DS
I have confidence in the policies of the Conservative party	AS	A	NC	D	DS
I am worried about my sex life	AS	A	NC	D	DS
I have sometimes considered taking my own life ...	AS	A	NC	D	DS
I am happy in my job	AS	A	NC	D	DS
I think the practice of homosexuality is wrong ...	AS	A	NC	D	DS

YMCAAI1/LJF78

	Agree Strongly	Agree	Not Certain	Disagree	Disagree Strongly
I think there should be more counselling facilities for young people in London	AS	A	NC	D	DS
I think speed limits should be strictly obeyed ...	AS	A	NC	D	DS
I think private medicine should be abolished ...	AS	A	NC	D	DS
What people think of me is important to me ...	AS	A	NC	D	DS
I think it is wrong to use marijuana (hash or pot)	AS	A	NC	D	DS
I think the trade unions have too much power ...	AS	A	NC	D	DS
Sometimes I have taken advantage of people ...	AS	A	NC	D	DS
It is not wrong to travel without a ticket if you are not caught	AS	A	NC	D	DS
I have found it helpful to talk about my problems with a minister of religion	AS	A	NC	D	DS
I hate London	AS	A	NC	D	DS
I think it is wrong for an unmarried couple to live together	AS	A	NC	D	DS
I often worry about my work	AS	A	NC	D	DS
I tend to be a lonely person	AS	A	NC	D	DS
I take an active part in church	AS	A	NC	D	DS

	Agree Strongly	Agree	Not Certain	Disagree	Disagree Strongly
I am worried that I might have a breakdown ...	AS	A	NC	D	DS
I often long for someone to turn to for advice ...	AS	A	NC	D	DS
I have found it helpful to talk about my problems with my father	AS	A	NC	D	DS
I think that it is all too easy to get mixed up with drugs in a place like London	AS	A	NC	D	DS
I feel my life has a sense of purpose	AS	A	NC	D	DS
I think it is wrong to use heroin	AS	A	NC	D	DS
I believe in my horoscope	AS	A	NC	D	DS
My appearance is important to me	AS	A	NC	D	DS
I am concerned about the risk of nuclear war ...	AS	A	NC	D	DS
Having a good time is more important than anything else	AS	A	NC	D	DS
I read a newspaper nearly every day	AS	A	NC	D	DS
I have confidence in the policies of the Liberal party	AS	A	NC	D	DS
Sometimes I have been jealous of others	AS	A	NC	D	DS
I take an active part in politics	AS	A	NC	D	DS

YMCAAI1/LJF78

	Agree Strongly	Agree	Not Certain	Disagree	Disagree Strongly
I think it is wrong to become drunk	AS	A	NC	D	DS
From time to time I feel I need to talk my problems over with someone	AS	A	NC	D	DS
I think religious education should be taught in schools	AS	A	NC	D	DS
I believe that luck plays an important part in my life	AS	A	NC	D	DS
I often long for someone to turn to for affection	AS	A	NC	D	DS
I am worried about my debts	AS	A	NC	D	DS
There is nothing wrong in bringing an extra bottle of spirits through the customs if you are not caught	AS	A	NC	D	DS
I think clergy are underpaid for the job they do	AS	A	NC	D	DS
I am concerned about the possibility of an invasion from outer space	AS	A	NC	D	DS
I feel no one knows me	AS	A	NC	D	DS
I have found it helpful to talk about my problems with a trained counsellor	AS	A	NC	D	DS
I find life really worth living	AS	A	NC	D	DS
I believe there is intelligent life on other planets	AS	A	NC	D	DS
Spending money is important to me	AS	A	NC	D	DS

	Agree Strongly	Agree	Not Certain	Disagree	Disagree Strongly
I think car workers are underpaid for the job they do	AS	A	NC	D	DS
There is nothing wrong with drinking and driving if you can get away with it	AS	A	NC	D	DS
I often think of moving away from England to find better prospects elsewhere	AS	A	NC	D	DS
My home and family are important to me	AS	A	NC	D	DS
I have never stolen anything in my life	AS	A	NC	D	DS
I am concerned about the problems of unemployment	AS	A	NC	D	DS
I think immigration into Britain should be restricted	AS	A	NC	D	DS
I think the nationalisation of industry is a good thing	AS	A	NC	D	DS
I would never discuss my problems with a minister of religion	AS	A	NC	D	DS
I want to get to the top in my work	AS	A	NC	D	DS
I believe in life after death	AS	A	NC	D	DS
I think that London has a lot more to offer the young person than other cities	AS	A	NC	D	DS
I think nurses are underpaid for the job they do	AS	A	NC	D	DS
I am always willing to admit when I make a mistake	AS	A	NC	D	DS

YMCAAI1/LJF78

	Agree Strongly	Agree	Not Certain	Disagree	Disagree Strongly
I have found it helpful to talk about my problems with my mother	AS	A	NC	D	DS
I like to have a lot of people around me	AS	A	NC	D	DS
Making money is important to me	AS	A	NC	D	DS
The church seems irrelevant for life today ...	AS	A	NC	D	DS
I believe in God	AS	A	NC	D	DS
I think tax returns should be filled in with complete honesty	AS	A	NC	D	DS
I would rather buy a British car than one made in another country	AS	A	NC	D	DS
I often watch sport in my leisure time	AS	A	NC	D	DS
I believe that it is becoming too easy to obtain a divorce	AS	A	NC	D	DS
I think that it is all too easy to get mixed up with prostitution in a place like London	AS	A	NC	D	DS
I think miners are underpaid for the job they do	AS	A	NC	D	DS
I am worried that I might get cancer	AS	A	NC	D	DS
I think the common market is a good thing	AS	A	NC	D	DS
I believe that there is too much violence on television	AS	A	NC	D	DS

YMCAAI1/LJF78

	Agree Strongly	Agree	Not Certain	Disagree	Disagree Strongly
My work is important to me	AS	A	NC	D	DS
I find crowds oppressive	AS	A	NC	D	DS
I am worried about the world situation	AS	A	NC	D	DS
It makes no difference which political party is in power	AS	A	NC	D	DS
Sometimes I feel resentful when I don't get my own way	AS	A	NC	D	DS
I think suicide is a sin	AS	A	NC	D	DS
I believe that the health service is becoming more inefficient	AS	A	NC	D	DS
I think it is important to work hard	AS	A	NC	D	DS
I have never broken my promise	AS	A	NC	D	DS
I am concerned about the rate of inflation ...	AS	A	NC	D	DS
I would rather go on social security than get a job I don't like doing	AS	A	NC	D	DS
I think too much economic power is in the hands of multinational corporations	AS	A	NC	D	DS
It is important for me to own my own house ...	AS	A	NC	D	DS
I have enjoyed filling in this questionnaire ...	AS	A	NC	D	DS

YMCAAI1/LJF78

HAVE YOU ANY HELPFUL COMMENTS YOU WOULD LIKE TO MAKE ABOUT THIS

QUESTIONNAIRE OR THE WORK OF LONDON CENTRAL YMCA

T H A N K   Y O U   F O R   Y O U R   H E L P

Index